Pitlochry Fe

presents

FAN FARE

A Collection of Recipes
from Friends of Pitlochry Festival Theatre
with an Introduction by
His Grace the Duke of Atholl

Illustrated by Ferelith Molteno

Sold in aid of the Pitlochry Festival
New Theatre Project

First published October 1978

ISBN 0 9506349 0 5

Set in 'Monotype' Times New Roman, series 327 and
printed at The Roundwood Press, Kineton,
in the County of Warwick, England

CONTENTS

ACKNOWLEDGMENTS

I would very much like to thank everyone who parted with their own special and favourite recipes for this book. I am sorry that it has not been possible to thank everyone personally.

I have been quite overwhelmed by the number of really splendid recipes which have come in. It has been a tremendous task selecting them – and so many good ones have had to be left out, owing to space, that I am hoping to use them in a companion book later.

In particular I am very grateful indeed to Mary Horsfall, for endless days of typing, and for helping in the final selection – and also to Ferelith Molteno for so generously giving her lovely illustrations with their background of local Perthshire scenes.

Barbara Liddell

EXPLANATION OF SYMBOLS

The symbols used in this book are:-

- E Economical
- (crown) Extravagant
- F Can be deep frozen
- NF Cannot be deep frozen

Time taken to make is preparation time only

All temperatures given are in degrees F.

INTRODUCTION

BLAIR CASTLE
BLAIR ATHOLL
PERTHSHIRE

Two of the great pleasures in life must be going to the theatre and eating a delicious dinner – in this book we have the two combined. Every time you pull this book from its shelf and make up one of its marvellous recipes, you will be reminded that thereby you (or perhaps a friend) have supported the Pitlochry Festival Theatre and brought the day nearer when it will be able to move into its new premises.

I would like to congratulate Barbara Liddell on obtaining recipes from so many friends of the theatre, and securing such a well balanced selection. Although I am no cook, it makes my mouth water just to read them, (whether it would if I tried to execute them is a different matter); but I am sure that you and your families will obtain many hours of happy eating as a result of this book.

Atholl.

PRECIOUS PUDDING

Take what you have of prosperity, no matter how little it be, raised with the leaves of thankfulness. It will increase to 3 times 3. Then put in some hospitality and a quantity of goodwill, a goodly portion of cheerfulness gives a pleasanter flavour still. Sweeten it well with charity, be sure and use plenty of that, for lacking this one ingredient the whole will be tasteless and flat. Spice it with fun and merriment and with many a timely jest, then bake it on the family hearth, of all places that is the best. When served with the sauce of kindness, 'tis a pudding fit for a king. For it cannot be bought or paid for – it is far too precious a thing.

Canadian recipe
Mrs T. G. Donald, Pitlochry

I guessed my pepper, my soup was too hot;
I guessed my water, it dried in the pot.
I guessed my salt, and what do you think?
For the rest of the day we did nothing but drink.
I guessed my sugar, my sauce was too sweet,
And thus by guessing I spoilt our treat.
So now I guess nothing, for cooking by guesses
Will ruin all skill and produce only messes.

From an old South African cookery book
Mrs Michael Riddell, Glenlyon

HOT & COLD
STARTERS

NF GUACOMOLE

2 ripe avocados
2 tomatoes, skinned
1 onion, chopped
1 teaspoon basil
3 tablespoons olive oil
2 tablespoons mayonnaise
juice of a lemon
4 drops tabasco
salt, pepper

Mash the avocados, mix in the mayonnaise and lemon juice. Slowly add the olive oil. Then add chopped onion and basil. Chop tomato and add, and finally the tabasco and salt and pepper to taste.
Keep one of the avocado pips and place it in the middle of the dip. It will stop the avocado from turning black.

5-10 mins
Serves 8-10

Jenny Abramsky, London

E AUBERGINE DIP

Take a large aubergine and burn the skin off it over a low light on top of the stove. When the aubergine is soft, wash skin right off it under running cold water. With a wooden spoon beat the aubergine to a pulp. Add salt and 1 crushed garlic clove. Gradually add drops of olive oil as carefully as if making a mayonnaise. Add juice of ½ lemon.

At this point the dip can be served – but it is even nicer if you go on.
In another dish take 2 tablespoons tahina cream. Mix very slowly alternately water and lemon juice until the mixture just runs off a spoon.
Now mix this mixture with the aubergine mixture.

20 mins
Serves 10

Old Turkish recipe
Jenny Abramsky, London

E NF SPINACH DIP

1 carton sour cream
3 tablespoons mayonnaise
juice of 1 lemon
salt, pepper
$\frac{1}{2}$lb. chopped frozen spinach
$1\frac{1}{2}$ teaspoons dill weed
1 small onion, chopped
1 tablespoon parsley, chopped

Thaw spinach, then mix all ingredients in a bowl and chill in the fridge for half an hour.
Serve as a dip with either celery stalks or heated pitta (Greek) bread.

5-10 mins
Serves 6-8

Jenny Abramsky, London

E NF OLIVE AND MUSHROOM DIP

$\frac{1}{4}$lb. black pitted olives, chopped
$\frac{1}{4}$lb. button mushrooms, chopped
1 carton natural yoghurt
1 carton sour cream
1 small onion, finely chopped
1 tablespoon white wine vinegar
juice of the olives
salt, pepper

Mix all the ingredients together and chill. Serve as a dip with Mexican taco chips, or ritz crackers.

10 mins
Serves 10

Own invention
Jenny Abramsky, London

E NF FRESH SPINACH STARTER

1½ lb. washed and trimmed fresh spinach
9 sliced fresh mushrooms
¼ lb. cooked crumbled bacon
small can mandarin oranges
1 large ripe avocado
French dressing made with lemon

Tear spinach into bite-sized pieces. Mix spinach, mushrooms, and half bacon and oranges together in bowl. Just before serving slice and add avocado.
Toss with dressing and decorate with remaining bacon and oranges.

10 mins
Serves 6

Italian recipe
Miss Ann Dixon, London

NF TUNA FISH SALAD

2 cans tuna fish, drained
spring onions, finely chopped
celery, finely chopped
1 or 2 apples, peeled and chopped
½ cucumber, peeled, deseeded and chopped
mayonnaise
¼ pawpaw chopped (tinned will do)
green pepper, finely chopped
parsley
lemon juice

Mix all together and serve in small glasses. Tinned fruit salad, drained, can be used instead of pawpaw.

20 mins
Serves 6

Mrs T. Rossaak, Johannesburg

MUSHROOMS IN GARLIC BUTTER

6 oz. unsalted butter
2 small cloves garlic
$\frac{3}{4}$ level teaspoon salt
$\frac{3}{4}$ oz. onion
1 small lemon
pepper
nutmeg (optional)
chopped parsley
2 oz. fresh breadcrumbs
1 lb. button mushrooms
butter for frying

Put the 6 oz. butter into bowl and cream it with wooden spoon. Add garlic crushed with salt, the onion finely chopped, lemon rind and juice, pepper, nutmeg (if used), parsley and breadcrumbs. Form the mixture into a cylinder, wrap it and chill in fridge.
Wash and dry mushrooms, fry until half cooked. Lift them out and put on one side.
Just before dinner divide mushrooms into 6 small dishes. Cover with slices of garlic butter and put under *very* hot grill until brown on top. Serve immediately with French bread.

Serves 6 *Mrs A. G. Godson, Headley, Hants*

NF

GRAPEFRUIT ASTORIA

2 grapefruit
1 teacup shelled shrimps
2 tablespoons mayonnaise
chopped parsley
paprika
pepper

Halve the grapefruit and remove the segments. Mix shrimps and grapefruit flesh and toss in mayonnaise. Line the grapefruit shells with lettuce, pile the shrimp mixture on to them.
Sprinkle with chopped parsley and decorate with paprika pepper.

20 mins
Serves 4 *Mrs W. S. Falconer, Burnside Hotel, Pitlochry*

GROUSE CLARET COCKTAIL

1½ pints tomato juice
2-3 tablespoons water
1 teaspoon white pepper
pinch garlic salt
orange and lemon wedges
1 teaspoon celery salt
1 teaspoon Worcester sauce
1 oz. gelatine
2 cans consommé
chopped chives

Soften ½ oz. gelatine in hot water. Put all other ingredients in pan and warm through to boiling point. Mix in dissolved gelatine and place in shallow container to set.
Dissolve the second ½ oz. gelatine in 2-3 tablespoons water and add 2 cans consommé. Pour into another shallow container to set. If necessary add more gelatine in hot weather.
Just before serving cut both jellies into cubes and arrange in chilled dishes. Garnish with orange and lemon wedges and sprinkle with chopped chives.

George Cameron, Craigard Hotel, Boat of Garten

CUCUMBER AND COTTAGE CHEESE MOUSSE

½ cucumber
3 tablespoons white wine vinegar
pinch castor sugar
8 oz. cottage cheese
salt, pepper
½ oz. powdered gelatine
¼ pint double cream
2 egg whites
parsley

Peel and dice half a cucumber very finely and mix with vinegar and sugar. Leave it to absorb flavours.
Beat up cottage cheese till smooth, add white pepper and salt to taste. Melt gelatine in 3 tablespoons of hot water, and when cool stir gently into the cottage cheese mixture. Then add the well drained cucumber.

When it is beginning to set fold in stiffly whipped cream, and then the egg whites stiffly whipped.

Put in soufflé dish and leave in fridge to set. Garnish with parsley.

Serves 6

Mrs J. Swanson, Denholm

E F CUCUMBER MOUSSE

1 large cucumber
salt
2 x 8 oz. or 227 g. cartons cottage cheese
¼ pint or 125 ml. mayonnaise or soured cream
6 tablespoons cold water
½ oz. powdered gelatine
lemon juice or wine vinegar
maybe a little green colouring
watercress to garnish

Peel the cucumber, cut in half lengthways and remove seeds. Chop cucumber flesh and place in colander. Sprinkle with salt, leave 1 hour to draw moisture. Drain well and press gently on cloth to dry.

Press cottage cheese through sieve into mixing basin. Blend with the mayonnaise or soured cream.

Measure water in bowl, sprinkle on gelatine. Allow to soak, then stir over low heat in a saucepan a quarter filled with water, until dissolved. Cool. Stir into cottage cheese mixture. Add seasoning and vinegar or juice to sharpen flavour. Fold in cucumber. The green colouring is optional.

Pour into ring mould until firm. Turn out and arrange watercress in centre.

20-25 mins

Serves 6-8

Mrs A. G. Thomson, Broughty Ferry

CHILLED EGG MOUSSE

- 6 hard-boiled eggs
- ¼ pint mayonnaise
- 1 level dessertspoon gelatine
- 5 tablespoons cold water
- 2 heaped teaspoons prepared mustard
- ¼ pint savoury sauce
- dash dry sherry
- 1 large raw egg white
- salt
- pepper

Sieve egg yolks. Chop whites finely with knife, mix with mayonnaise and mustard. Dissolve gelatine, and mix all together. Stir in white sauce and add sherry if required. Whisk egg white very stiffly and fold into mixture. Turn into individual dishes and allow to set.

Garnish with asparagus, tomato, or as required. May be made the day before.

30 mins
Serves 8

Mrs J. A. R. Macphail, Ballinluig

♔ NF AVOCADO MOUSSE

- ¼ pint cold water
- ½ oz. powdered gelatine
- ¼ pint chicken stock
- 2 large avocado pears
- ½ large onion
- 2 teaspoons Worcester sauce
- ¼ pint mayonnaise
- ¼ pint double cream
- salt
- freshly milled pepper

Measure water into small saucepan, heat gently, sprinkle gelatine over, set aside for a few minutes. Gelatine will dissolve and mixture will become clear, but do not allow it to boil. Draw pan off heat, stir in stock and allow mixture to cool.

Halve avocados, remove stones and scoop out flesh into a mixing basin, and mash with a fork until smooth. Grate onion finely on to a saucer and measure 1 teaspoon onion juice. Add juice to avocado, season with salt and freshly milled pepper, add Worcester sauce. Slowly pour in gelatine mixture and stir

until just beginning to thicken. Gently fold in mayonnaise and slightly whipped cream.
Pour into wetted 1½ pint mould or ring, chill until firm. Unmould just before eating, and serve with prawns and either oil and vinegar dressing or mayonnaise.

1 hour
Serves 6 *The Marchioness of Aberdeen and Temair, Aberdeen*

E ASPARAGUS MOUSSE

1 tin asparagus tips
1 tin asparagus soup
½ oz. gelatine
½ pint cream
salt, pepper
sherry glass white wine

Drain tips. Heat liquid and mix gelatine to dissolve. When cool beat in cream, seasoning and wine.
Serve in individual glasses or one larger bowl. When set decorate with asparagus tips.

10-15 mins
Serves 8 *Mrs Jean D. R. Crystal, Aberfeldy*

F MOUSSE MIMOSA

¼ pint aspic jelly
6 hard-boiled eggs
2 tablespoons Worcester sauce
anchovy sauce
½ pint home-made mayonnaise
¼ pint cream
salt, pepper

Make aspic jelly and cool in fridge. Separate eggs, sieve yolks and chop whites. Mix well together. Lightly whip cream.
Add aspic jelly to egg mixture, stir in anchovy and Worcester sauces, pepper and salt. Stir in cream and mayonnaise. Put in dish and put back in fridge.
(See separate recipe for aspic jelly).

Serves 8 *Miss M. Douglas, Ballinluig*

NF FORDELL MOUSSE

1 pint double or whipping cream
6 oz. lump fish roe (mock caviare)
2 fresh lemons
seasoning

Whip the cream and gently stir in the lump fish roe, add seasoning. Serve in ramekin dishes with a quarter of fresh lemon and eat with toast and butter.

5 mins
Serves 8 *Nicholas Fairbairn, Q.C., M.P., House of Commons*

E F SMOKED HADDOCK MOUSSE

½ lb. smoked haddock, cooked and flaked
2 hard-boiled eggs, sliced
½ pint béchamel sauce made with 1 oz. butter, 1 oz. flour and ½ pint milk
¼ pint mayonnaise
½ oz. gelatine, dissolved in 3-4 tablesp. water
3 fl. oz. cream, lightly whipped
white pepper, salt, ground mace

Add the prepared fish and hard-boiled eggs to the béchamel sauce. Carefully blend in the dissolved and cooled gelatine. Stir in the mayonnaise, mace, pepper and salt to taste. Fold in the cream as the mixture starts to thicken.
Pour into a very lightly oiled ring mould or individual serving dishes. Cover and chill until set.
Turn out and decorate with cress. Serve on a bed of lettuce.
This should not be left in the deep freeze for more than two months.

20 mins
Serves 6-8 *Sir Douglas Haddow, Edinburgh*

E NF SHRIMP WHIZZ

1 can consommé
1 hard-boiled egg per person
1 tin shrimps
1 tablespoon cream (optional) – can be used to garnish
dash of sherry

Put hard-boiled eggs, consommé and shrimps through the liquidiser. Add cream, if wanted, and sherry, and put into one large dish or individual dishes.
This recipe should be done the day before it is wanted.

15 mins
Serves 6 *Mrs Ronald Crawford, Kinloch Rannoch*

NF HADDOCK MOUSSE

Cook 1 lb. smoked haddock in half pint of milk and water, with 1 onion, 1 carrot, parsley and a bouquet garni, and a few black peppercorns.
Make ½ pint mayonnaise and ½ pint béchamel sauce, using the haddock liquid. Dissolve ½ oz. gelatine in water or stock. Mix sauce, mayonnaise and cooked gelatine. Add 5 roughly-chopped hard-boiled eggs and rather coarsely flaked haddock. Mix together. Lastly add ¼ pint lightly whipped cream.
Garnish dish with sliced hard-boiled eggs in aspic jelly, and serve with brown bread and butter.

45 mins
Serves 6 *J. Douglas Hutchison, C.B.E., M.C., Aberfeldy*

SAVOURY STARTER

½ lb. smoked haddock fillets
¼ pint vinegar
¼ pint water
2 bay leaves
salt, pepper
few sprigs fresh parsley
1 onion, peeled and grated
1 chopped hard-boiled egg
¼ pint sour cream
1 packet lemon jelly, (dissolved in ¼ pint hot water)

Place smoked haddock in a shallow pan with water, vinegar, bay leaves and seasoning. Bring to the boil. Simmer over low heat for about 8 mins. Remove bay leaves and reserve liquid. Skin and flake fish. Add onion, egg and sour cream to fish and mix well.
Strain reserved cooking liquid into dissolved jelly. Stir into fish mixture, reserving ¼ pint liquid for top.
Turn fish mixture into 6 individual dishes and allow to set in fridge. Decorate top with parsley. Carefully spoon two tablespoons of jelly over each dish. Then return to fridge to set.

20 mins
Serves 6

Miss Betty J. Brydone, Pitlochry

E MARINADED KIPPER FILLETS

1 large packet kipper fillets (frozen are perfectly all right)
1 small onion
1 bay leaf
lemon slices
watercress
1 teaspoon castor sugar
1 teaspoon prepared mustard
3 tablespoons white wine vinegar
4 tablespoons olive oil
salt, pepper

Skin kipper fillets if necessary and arrange in bottom of shallow dish. Cover with onion rings and bay leaf. Mix together sugar, mustard, vinegar, olive oil, salt and pepper, pour over fillets. Cover dish and leave for 24 hours.

Drain the fillets and garnish with lemon slices and watercress. Leave the onion rings with the kipper fillets if you like the flavour. Serve with thin slices of brown bread and butter.

Serves 4 *Mrs A. G. Godson, Headley, Hants*

E F SMOKED TROUT PATE

- ¾ lb. minced smoked trout (or less)
- 4 oz. cream cheese (more or less according to taste)
- 1½ oz. melted butter
- ½ teaspoon onion juice (optional)
- lemon juice
- black pepper
- 4 tablespoons cream

Prepare minced trout and mix with ¾ oz. melted butter, cream cheese, onion juice, lemon juice, black pepper and cream. If too stiff add more cream until it is of pâté consistency. Put into dishes and seal tops with rest of melted butter.

We find this economical as we catch and smoke our own trout. However you can convert this pâté to your own taste and replace the trout with smoked mackerel, prawns, pieces of smoked salmon or mashed sardines.

10 mins

Serves 6-8 *Mrs Colin Stroyan, Killin*

MACKEREL PATE

½ lb. smoked mackerel fillets
2 teaspoons finely chopped chives
2 teaspoons lemon juice
pinch paprika
2 oz. butter
¼ lb. cream cheese
salt and pepper to taste

Pound the mackerel fillets and add chives, lemon juice and paprika. Add butter and cream cheese and cream with the fish mixture. Add seasoning if needed.
Put into avocado pear halves or hollowed-out green peppers, and garnish with finely chopped capers or sliced stuffed olives. Serve with brown bread and butter or toast.

10 mins

Serves 4 *Mrs Colin McGlashan, Pitlochry*

E

SMOKIE PATE

1 Arbroath smokie to 1 oz. melted butter
1 teaspoon whisky
salt, pepper

Allow half a fish to each person.
Slake fish from bone and pound till smooth. Add melted butter, salt and pepper, and whisky to taste. Turn into serving dish and leave to mature a few hours in fridge. Garnish with sprigs of parsley and serve with fingers of hot buttered toast.

15 mins *Mrs Tom Finlayson, Aberfeldy*

E CHICKEN LIVER PATE

$\frac{1}{2}$ lb. chicken livers
$\frac{1}{4}$ pint double cream
1 clove garlic
1 tablespoon brandy
1 oz. butter
tinned consommé (optional)
salt, pepper
mixed spice or mace

Cook the livers gently in butter, remove whilst they are still slightly pink. Liquidise or put through food mill. Season with salt and pepper and a little mixed spice or mace. Stir in crushed garlic and brandy. Whip the cream and fold in. Put in fridge overnight.

The next day cover with thin layer of consommé and decorate with stuffed olives if liked. Chill again. Serve with toast.

Mrs A. G. Godson, Headley, Hants

E NF PATE MAISON

$\frac{1}{2}$ lb. liver
1 lb. pork
salt, pepper
chopped chives
1 egg
dash of brandy
bay leaves

Ask your butcher to mince meat very finely. Stir together in bowl and add salt, pepper, chopped chives and a beaten egg. Add a dash of brandy if you like.

Turn into medium oven dish and garnish with 2 or 3 bay leaves. Cover tightly, if possible using dish with hole in the lid for steam to escape. Place in a roasting tin half filled with water in moderate oven (gas mark 4), and cook for $2\frac{1}{2}$ hours. Remove lid towards end of cooking period to allow to brown slightly on top. Immediately on removal from oven place a weight or heavy object on top of the meat. Leave weighted overnight to get completely cold. Serve sliced, with salads.

15 mins
Serves 8

Recipe comes from Anjou, France
Mrs T. S. Drew, Coupar Angus

♔ F CHICKEN LIVER PATE

18 oz. chicken liver
11 oz. butter
salt, pepper
plenty of mixed spice
2 glasses of very good port

Boil port. Add chicken liver to port and continue cooking for 3 mins, but *no longer*. Switch off heat and leave to cool. Then strain, keeping port.
Chop liver finely, add softened butter, salt, pepper and spice. Liquidise *briefly* with port. Put in a dish, cover with foil, put a plate on top and then a heavy weight. *If kept covered with foil it will stay pink and not go brown. This is extravagant but absolutely super.*

Madame Eliane Goldbleue, Paris

E F CHICKEN LIVER PATE

1 medium onion
1 clove garlic
3 oz. butter
8 oz. chicken livers
1 dessertspoon brandy
parsley
bay leaf
few sprigs thyme
seasoning

Chop onion, crush garlic, soften in 1 oz. butter. Add livers and sauter for 2-3 mins. Sprinkle with chopped herbs and seasoning. Cook again for about 1 min. Cool. Either liquidise or chop and pound. Stir in remaining butter, melted, and the brandy. Pack into a mould and chill.
I usually buy a 5lb. bag of frozen livers from a freezer centre and make up 10 *times the recipe. I then freeze it in ½ lb. margarine tubs which give* 4 *good servings in each. This gives me ready-made dinner starters which keep well in the freezer.*

15 mins
Serves 6

Mrs A. Henderson, Aberfeldy

F GROUSE PATE

4 old grouse	whisky
½ lb. butter	salt, pepper, mace

Roast grouse in baking tin with ½ lb. butter, covering with foil so that no steam can escape. Cook in slow oven at gas mark 3 for one hour. When cold skin, and discard skin. Remove all meat from the bone and mince three times, or liquidise till smooth. Add juices from pan. Add salt and pepper to taste, a liqueur glass of whisky and ½ teaspoon ground mace.
Pack into ramekin dishes. When cold cover with clarified butter.

Mrs Barbara Liddell, Pitlochry

F GROUSE PATE

1 lb. fat pork belly	1 clove garlic (optional)
2 old grouse, uncooked	12 black peppercorns
1 small coffee cup dry white wine	3 dozen juniper berries
	¼ teaspoon ground mace
2 tablespoons brandy	1 oz. fat bacon
salt	

Mince the pork and the meat off the grouse. Chop half the bacon, mix thoroughly with the wine, brandy, herbs and seasoning (½ to 1 dessertspoon salt will probably be needed). Leave to stand for about 2 hours. Turn into baking tin and cover the top with remaining strips of bacon.
Cook in oven at 310° for 1¼ hours, standing the tin in water. The pâté is ready when the sides of the meat come away from the tin.
This recipe was tested at Blair Castle and Ardchattan Priory. It is an economical recipe if old grouse are available.

Serves 10 *Lt. Col. R. Campbell-Preston, O.B.E., M.C., Connel*

E F TERRINE OF VENISON LIVER PATE

1 venison liver – hind's liver preferable, though stag's will do if early on (before mid-September)

½ lb. streaky bacon	bayleaf, salt, pepper
1 medium onion	glass sherry and a little stock
1 clove garlic	2 eggs

Slice liver and chop onion slightly. Put through mincer with bacon and garlic. Add rest of the ingredients and pour into well greased terrine. Any left over can be put into aluminium foil dishes. Bake in medium oven until well cooked (about one hour). *Do not freeze for longer than about 2 months.*

10 mins
Serves 8 *Mrs Danvers Valentine, Aberfeldy*

E F STAG'S LIVER PATE

1½ lb. stag's liver	¾ pint thin cream
10 anchovies	pepper
½ lb. fat bacon	a *little* salt
4 eggs	strip of lining fat if not using
bay leaf	foil inside loaf tin

Put all ingredients through chopper or mincer until smooth. Pour into loaf tin or pâté dish. Stand container in tin or dish containing about an inch of water, and bake in middle of moderate oven for about an hour. When cool decorate with bay leaf and one or two anchovies and cover with thin layer of melted butter.

15 mins
Serves 10-12 *Mrs Angus Stroyan, Killin*

E F POTTED GAME

10 oz. cooked game
pinch each of dried marjoram, thyme and mace
3 oz. unsalted butter
salt
black pepper

Finely mince the chopped meat. Season to taste with the herbs, salt and pepper. Cook in 2 oz. of butter for about 5 mins. Pack the meat into a jar and leave to cool.

Heat the remaining butter until bubbling, strain through muslin and pour over the meat. Leave the jar in a cool place to set.

The potted meat can be used for sandwiches, with hot toast or with a salad.

15 mins — This is a 16th Century way to use up left-overs

Serves 4 — *Miss E. M. Honeyman, Ballinluig*

E F POTTED GROUSE

2 old grouse
1 medium carrot
1 medium onion
2 oz. streaky bacon
bunch of mixed herbs
salt, pepper
4 oz. clarified butter

Clean grouse, slice carrot and onion and chop bacon. Put bacon into a pan and heat until the fat runs. Add chopped carrot and onion and cook gently until golden. Transfer to casserole and add the herbs, salt and pepper, and the grouse. Cover, preferably with stock, or failing that with water, and replace lid. Cook at 300° or gas mark 2, for 2½ hours.

Remove pieces of onion and carrot. Remove meat from the grouse and put through mincer or electric blender, with the bacon. Pound to a paste with a little cooking liquid, press into a dish and cover with clarified butter.

Freshly ground black pepper is essential, and of course the grouse should be well hung to obtain the "gamey" flavour. The potted meat can be served with hot toast or fresh wholemeal bread, or used as a filling for baps for the hill.

30 mins — *Basil Death, Calvine*

E F CARROT PATE

1 lb. carrots
½ lb. cream cheese
1 tablespoon chopped chives
1 tablespoon chopped parsley
salt and freshly ground black pepper to taste

Wash and peel carrots, chop roughly and boil for 10 mins in boiling water. Strain and mash with potato masher, i.e. not completely mashed. Gradually work in cheese with fork, season to taste. Add chopped chives and parsley. Refrigerate. Serve with hot buttered toast or wholemeal bread.
Comment by eight year old granddaughter: 'What a delicious way to eat carrots, Grannie'.

20 mins
Serves 8

Mrs R. S. Masterton, Aberfeldy

E F CUCUMBER PATE

1 cucumber
juice of 1 lemon
1 packet gelatine
2 tablespoons water
8 oz. cottage or Philadelphia cheese
1 small onion
seasoning

Grate cucumber coarsely. Mash cheese, blend in cucumber with fork.
Combine lemon juice, water and gelatine, and dissolve thoroughly over hot water. Add cucumber and cheese mixture and mix in finely grated onion. Season to taste. Chill in fridge for at least 2 hours.
The mixture can be chilled either in a ring or in a bowl, or put into individual ramekin dishes. The latter is the easiest for serving and one is spared having to turn the pâté out of the ring.

30 mins
Serves 6

Mrs Guy Lorimer, Pitlochry

♔ NF PRAWN AVOCADO DISH

1 oz. butter or marg
1 oz. flour
½ pint milk
¼ pint cream
2 avocados
6 oz. prawns
3 oz. gruyère cheese
salt, pepper
2 oz. brown bread
1 oz. Cheddar cheese

Melt fat in saucepan and blend in flour. Add milk slowly and add grated gruyère cheese. Flavour, add cream.
Liquidise bread and Cheddar cheese, and toast slowly in hot oven for 10-15 mins, gas mark 4.
Add chopped avocado and prawns to sauce and heat together. Serve in avocado dishes and sprinkle breadcrumb mixture on top.

15-20 mins Own recipe
Serves 6 *Mrs J. L. Morison, Perth*

E SCAMPI IN CREAM

2 lb. scampi
1 tablespoon butter
salt
½ pint double cream
brandy
white pepper

If the scampi is frozen allow to thaw in packet and preserve juices and water that form.
Put the butter in a large pan and heat gently until melted. Add scampi and juices. Heat moderately until scampi is white (about 3 mins). Remove from heat. Remove scampi from pan, leaving butter and juices. Add cream, seasoning, boil fast until thick. Return scampi to sauce. Salt to taste. Add ½ tablespoon brandy, fold scampi into sauce to prevent breaking fish to pieces.
Heat for a few seconds and serve.

15 mins
Serves 6 *Paul White, The Pine Trees Hotel, Pitlochry*

E NF FISH STARTER

1 tin salmon (drained) or 8 oz. cooked fresh salmon
½ pint white sauce
2 tablespoons chopped parsley
4 tomatoes, peeled and sliced
salt and pepper to taste
4 oz. breadcrumbs

Put salmon in basin and mash. Stir parsley into white sauce and add salmon. Season to taste.
Grease an ovenproof dish and put a layer of salmon, tomatoes and crumbs alternately.
Top with crumbs and knobs of butter. Cook in medium hot oven for 30 mins.

10 mins
Serves 4-6 *Mrs D. Hattersley Smith, Killiecrankie Hotel*

E CHAMPIGNONS FARCIS

12 large mushrooms, wiped
1 teaspoon salt
½ teaspoon freshly ground black pepper
1 tablespoon melted butter
2 tablespoons butter
1 tablespoon flour
2 shallots or spring onions, finely chopped
4 fl. oz. single cream
3 tablespoons chopped fresh parsley
1½ tablespoons grated Parmesan cheese

This is a recipe for mushrooms filled with a cream and parsley mixture and topped with cheese.
Preheat oven to fairly hot, 375° or gas mark 5. Remove stems from mushrooms and set them aside. Season mushroom caps with ½ teaspoon salt and ¼ teaspoon black pepper and, using a pastry brush, coat them with the melted butter. Arrange them, hollow side up, in a shallow baking dish.

With sharp knife chop mushroom stems finely. Wrap them in kitchen paper towels and twist to extract as much juice from them as possible. In a medium sized frying pan melt the 2 tablespoons butter over moderate heat. When the foam subsides add the chopped mushroom stems and shallots or spring onions. Sauter them together for 4 to 5 minutes. Reduce the heat to low and, stirring constantly, add flour. Cook for 1 minute. Remove pan from heat and stir in the cream, a little at a time. When sauce is smooth and all ingredients are blended, return the pan to heat and simmer sauce for 2-3 mins, or until it has thickened. Stir in parsley and remaining salt and pepper and mix well. Remove pan from heat and spoon a little of the mixture into each of the prepared mushroom caps. Top each mushroom with a little grated cheese. Place dish in oven and bake the mushrooms for 15 mins or until they are tender and the stuffing is lightly browned on top. Remove from oven and serve.

30 mins
Serves 4 *Mrs David Hayter, Methven*

F HAGGIS "STILLAIG"

approx. 1½ lb. fresh haggis
scant 1 oz. butter
3 tablespoons chopped fresh chives
freshly ground black pepper
pinch salt
at least ½ gill whisky
approx. 6 tablespoons fresh cream (preferably single)

Skin haggis if necessary, warm 6 ramekins in oven and turn on the grill.

Very gently heat haggis in a stewpan with the butter, stirring to avoid burning. When hot add ⅔ of the chives, and pepper and salt to taste. Then add the whisky.

This will flame mildly. When flame dies, transfer to ramekins and pour over the cream (approx. 1 tablespoon per ramekin) and brown lightly under grill without allowing it to dry out.

Remove from grill, garnish with the remaining chives and serve at once with plenty of hot buttered brown toast.
N.B. More whisky may be added if required after removing from grill. This is a starter to turn even the most stubborn English head!

10 mins Original Loch Tummel Hotel recipe 1976
Serves 6 *Andrew Mackenzie, Loch Tummel Hotel, Strathtummel*

Note: This was on the point of going to press when the typist saw that she had heated the haggis in a stewpan with the butler. The butler has now been retrieved and she apologises to him for any discomfort caused.

E NF MOCK ESCARGOTS

Select 2 dozen small open mushrooms and remove stalks. Prepare ½ lb. strong fresh garlic butter, using 6 large garlic cloves. Take a knife and fill mushrooms level with the garlic butter. Arrange on a large grilling dish with the butter uppermost and grill under a hot flame for 5 mins or less.
Sprinkle with a little chopped parsley and serve as a starter. They are delicious and just like snails.

15 mins
Serves 3 *Paul White, The Pine Trees Hotel, Pitlochry*

F QUICK COLD TOMATO SOUP

1 tin consommé
2 tins tomato juice, or sieved tinned tomatoes
1 can concentrated frozen orange juice
pepper, garlic powder, chives, marjoram.

Mix all together, adding seasonings to taste. Serve chilled. Dilute with cold stock if necessary.

5 mins
Serves 6-8 *Mrs J. C. Stormonth Darling, North Berwick*

E NF LEBANESE SOUP

1 clove garlic, crushed
salt, pepper
1 carton plain yoghurt, large
1 carton single cream, large
¼ cucumber, finely sliced
handful of fresh chopped mint
2 oz. shrimps

Mix all ingredients together, chill in fridge.
Before serving decorate with chopped chives and parsley.

10 mins
Serves 4 *Lady Keith, Strathtummel*

NF ICED AVOCADO PEAR SOUP

3 avocados
2 chicken cubes
½ pint light cream
1 pint water
a little milk
seasoning if necessary

Dissolve chicken cubes in a little hot water, add remainder of water and the milk. Peel and stone fruit. Put into liquidiser, adding some of the chicken stock, and whizz until very fine and creamy.
Whip cream slightly and add all ingredients together, seasoning if necessary. Chill in fridge for at least 2 hours.

15 mins
Serves 6 *The Right Hon. Anthony Stodart, North Berwick*

E GASPACHIO

1 tin tomato paste (3½″ high)
1 cucumber
¼ green pepper
3 whites of hard-boiled eggs

All above ingredients should be chopped finely.
Add:

⅓ cup olive oil
3 cups tomato juice
a little chilli sauce according to hotness preferred

Mix everything together and serve very very cold.

Serves 6 *Mrs R. S. Stewart-Wilson, Tulliemet*

ICED CURRY SOUP

1 oz. butter
1 medium onion
1 tablespoon curry paste
1 oz. plain flour
1¾ pints chicken stock
strip of lemon rind
1 bay leaf

¼ pint boiling water
1 tablespoon ground almonds
1 tablespoon coconut
1 dessertspoon arrowroot
1 tablespoon cold stock or water

Cream topping:

1 glass port
1 teaspoon curry powder
1 dessertspoon apricot jam
4 tablespoons double cream

Melt ¾ oz. butter, add chopped onion, cook slowly till just turning colour. Add curry paste and a dusting of flour, fry gently for 4-5 mins. Stir in remaining butter, blend in rest of the flour and the stock. Bring to the boil.

Add bay leaf and lemon rind and simmer for 20 mins. Strain, return to rinsed pan, continue simmering for 10-15 mins. Meanwhile pour the ¼ pint boiling water over the almonds and coconut and leave for 30 mins. Then squeeze this mixture in muslin and add the resulting liquid to the soup. Mix arrowroot with the cold stock, add to the pan and re-boil. Strain again. Allow to cool and then chill.

To make topping mix port and curry powder. Simmer till reduced to half the quantity and leave till cold. Mix in the jam. Squeeze mixture through muslin. Reserve the liquid and stir into it the lightly whipped cream. Serve the soup in cups, with a spoonful of the topping on the top. *Takes ages to make, but is a super party dish.*

Serves 4 *Mrs Alice M. Macnab of Macnab, Killin*

E BEAUTIFUL BEETROOT BORTSCH

1 medium onion
2 tins consommé
1 medium jar baby beetroots in sweet vinegar *or* home grown beets soaked in sweet vinegar
cream or sour cream or plain yoghurt
chives or parsley

Chill soup cans overnight. Chop beets into matchsticks, fry onion gently in butter.
Put consommé into bowl, add onion, beets and juice. Whisk gently with fork. Re-chill. Serve with blob of cream, sour cream or yoghurt, and with chives or parsley.

10 mins
Serves 6

Mrs Donald Dunlop, Dunalastair

LEEK AND POTATO SOUP

5 medium sized potatoes
2 leeks
1 pint milk
salt, pepper

Boil potatoes in the usual way until soft, drain, place in liquidiser with 1 pint cold milk. Liquidise at top speed for 1 min. Clean and chop the 2 leeks and simmer gently in 2 cupfuls of salted water for 2 mins. Add the liquidised potatoes and milk to the cooked leeks. Heat, season with salt and pepper and serve garnished with chopped parsley.
This is a very economical and quickly made soup. The ingredients are simple, as are most ingredients of traditional Scottish recipes, and tastes even better if you collect the two leeks from your vegetable patch. Leeks can be planted in the autumn and be available throughout the winter – straight from the garden, and give a very special flavour to the soup.

Norman Renfrew, Provost, Perth & Kinross District Council, Perth

♔ NF VODKA CONSOMME "BIRDSHOT"

1 portion consommé (heated)
generous slug vodka

Combine, and enjoy.
Excellent in cold weather when you have been shooting, or for an evening party.

5 mins *Nicholas Fairbairn, Q.C., M.P., House of Commons*

E F LETTUCE SOUP

2 oz. butter or marg
1 large onion
1 large potato
2 large lettuces – those past their prime may be used
½ pint chicken stock (this may be made with stock cubes)
2 lumps sugar
nutmeg
milk

Wash lettuce thoroughly and chop. Melt butter or marg in large pan, add chopped onion and potato. Cook until soft, taking care not to let them brown. Add lettuce and stock and simmer for approx. 10 mins. Cool quickly by placing pan in cold water. Liquidise when cool.
At this stage the soup may be placed in containers and put in freezer, where it will keep for up to 12 months. When required for use the soup should be brought to boiling point, and sugar, nutmeg and seasoning added. Finally bring to required consistency by adding milk and bring back to boil. Remove from heat immediately.

20 mins
Serves 6 *Mrs Olive Holden, Strathtay*

E F TOMATO AND ORANGE SOUP

4 medium onions
6 oz. butter
4 oz. flour
1½ pints orange juice
(fresh, frozen or canned)
1½ lb. tomatoes
tabasco, Worcester sauce, salt, pepper, brown sugar, all to taste
dash of tomato purée

Chop onions fairly finely and cook until soft in the butter. Add flour and cook for two minutes. Add orange juice gradually, until smooth and thickened. Skin tomatoes and chop roughly. Add to soup.
Season and add purée as needed.

Serves 8

Mrs David Yellowlees, Perth

E F TOMATO SOUP

1 lb. tomatoes
1 large onion, finely sliced
1 clove garlic, crushed
1 tablespoon olive oil
1 pint chicken stock
salt, pepper

Heat oil in large pan, add onion and garlic, fry till soft. Place tomatoes in boiling water for 30 seconds and then remove skins. Chop roughly and add to pan. Cook for 5 mins over low heat and add stock. Simmer for 15-20 mins till tomatoes are soft, then liquidise. Season with salt and pepper and serve piping hot, garnished with parsley or thin slices of lemon. May also be served cold.
This soup is ideal for using last season's tomatoes from the freezer.
Only 40 calories per serving.

30 mins
Serves 4

Mrs F. Carruthers, Moulin

E F VEGETABLE SOUP

1 lb. onions, sliced thinly
¾ lb. carrots, sliced thinly
1 lb. potatoes, diced
½ lb. mushrooms, quartered
½ lb. bacon, chopped
2 lb. firm tomatoes
6 pints good beef stock
salt, black pepper
chopped parsley

Place bacon in large pan over very gentle heat until fat melts, then add onions to cook very slowly. When almost brown add carrots, potatoes and mushrooms. Continue to heat gently, stirring frequently, for a further 7 mins.
Add stock, bring to the boil, cover and simmer for approx. 30 mins. Add the peeled and chopped tomatoes, salt and freshly ground black pepper, and cook for a further 10 mins.
Garnish with chopped parsley.

20 mins
Serves 12 *Mrs D. G. Rhind, Aberfeldy*

E F CURRIED BEETROOT SOUP

1 lb. raw beetroot
1 apple
1 onion
2-3 tomatoes
1 oz. butter
1 teaspoon curry powder
salt, pepper
1 bay leaf
1 dessertspoon sultanas
1½ pints stock
½ oz. flour
¼ pint milk

Peel beetroot, apple, onion and tomatoes, and chop small. Fry lightly without browning, in the butter. Add curry powder, seasoning, bay leaf, sultanas and stock and bring to the boil. Simmer gently until well cooked. Blend flour and milk. Add to the soup and remove bay leaf. Boil again and simmer for a few minutes before serving.

10 mins
Serves 6 *Mrs D. Sinclair, Perth*

E F MUTTON BROTH

1 lb. (or more) neck of mutton
1 lb. each of carrots and turnips
4 or 5 onions
½ cupful barley
salt

Using blunt end of knitting needle remove marrow from bone and discard. Place meat in pot and cover with cold water. Add washed barley and salt and bring to boil. Simmer for about one hour. Add one grated carrot. Cut up turnip and remaining carrots into chunks and, with the whole onions, add to soup. Simmer for about 1½ hours. Leave to cool overnight.
Next day remove fat and top up with water. Bring to the boil, lift out whole onions. Squash these and pour back into soup. Lift out the mutton and vegetables and use as the meat course.

Serves 4 *Mrs J. Panton, Larbert*

E GERMAN SOUP

½ lb. potatoes, cubed
2 carrots, cubed
1 leek, sliced
1 stick celery, sliced small
2 medium onions, chopped
7 oz. (or less) streaky bacon
½ oz. marg
1 beef stock cube
salt
pepper
¼ lb. salami

Melt marg in large saucepan, fry bacon. Then add carrots, leek, celery and onion and fry for 5 mins. Add 1 beef cube dissolved in 1 pint boiling water, add salt and pepper.
Boil, cover and simmer for 10 mins. Add potatoes, simmer 10 more mins. Dice ¼ lb. salami very small, add to the soup and simmer for a further 10 mins or until all the vegetables are cooked. This is a very filling and fairly thick soup. Add more stock cubes and water if preferred thinner.

30 mins
Serves 6 *Mrs John Horsfall, Kinloch Rannoch*

E F WATERCRESS SOUP

2 bunches watercress
2 oz. butter
3 oz. onions, finely chopped
1½ pints milk (or milk and water)
1½ level tablespoons flour
2 chicken stock cubes
2 tablespoons cream (optional)

Wash watercress, coarsely chop, remove any thick stalks. Melt the butter. Add watercress and onions and cook gently for 5-6 mins.
Boil the milk. Stir flour, stock cubes and boiling milk on to the watercress and onions. Cover and simmer for 15-20 mins. Liquidise soup or pass it through a fine sieve.
Reheat and serve, spooning, if liked, a little cream and croutons on each portion. To make croutons cut bread into small cubes, toss with butter and salt over fairly high heat until crisp and golden.

25 mins
Serves 6 *Clive Perry, Birmingham Repertory Theatre*

E F POTAGE A L'ORANGE

1½ pints water
1 cup lentils
2 lb. carrots
1 onion
2 chicken cubes
1 tin tomato soup
1 orange, sliced
cream to garnish

Scrape and chop carrots and put in water, add chopped onion and lentils and boil until soft enough to rub through sieve. Return to pan, add tin of soup and 2 chicken cubes. Bring to boil.
Serve in bowl with a slice of orange on top. Garnish with double cream, but if freezing omit cream until time of serving.

10 mins
Serves 6 *Mrs R. Begg, Bearsden*

VEGETABLE SOUP

Take some carrots, onion and celery. Chop into small pieces and fry gently in a little margarine. Add 1½ pints of water and 1 packet Cream of Chicken soup. Cook until vegetables are soft, put through liquidiser.

Re-heat, add salt and pepper to taste. Sprinkle on some dried herbs and add a little tabasco sauce to taste. Sprinkle with parsley or chopped chives. Serve with a dab of cream on top.

Sir Alexander Gibson, Glasgow

E F HUNGARIAN GULYAS SOUP

- 1½ oz. lard
- 2 medium onions
- 1 tablespoon paprika pepper
- 2 lb. beef
- ½ raw potato, grated
- 1 tablespoon tomato purée
- 4½ pints bone and vegetable stock
- 1 lb. potatoes
- 1 green pepper

For csipetke:

- 6 oz. flour
- 1 egg
- pinch salt

Fry finely chopped onions in lard to a golden colour, add paprika pepper, the beef cut into walnut-sized cubes and the grated raw potato. Cover and simmer for about 10 mins, stirring occasionally. Add tomato purée and half cupful stock. Simmer until meat is nearly cooked. Add remainder of stock, bring to the boil, add potatoes cut in small cubes. If available add some sliced green pepper.

Csipetke: Genuine Hungarian gulyas soup is garnished with csipetke. Make them as follows:

Sift flour into bowl, add egg and salt. Knead ingredients into a stiff dough. Flatten between palms of the hand and pinch into small bean-sized pieces. Add to the gulyas and boil slowly for 10 mins before serving.

20 mins Hungarian national dish
Serves 6-8 *Mrs John MacKay, Pitlochry*

E BOUILLABAISSE D'OEUFS

- 6 tablespoons olive oil
- 2 leeks (white part only), finely chopped
- 1 spanish onion, finely chopped
- 3 tomatoes, chopped – or 1 tin tomatoes
- 4 cloves garlic, mashed
- fennel (if available)
- 1 bouquet garni
- 1 piece orange peel
- 4 potatoes – thinly sliced
- turmeric
- seasoning
- water/stock to cover
- 1 egg per person

Sauter chopped leeks and onion in olive oil until transparent. Add tomatoes, garlic, fennel, bouquet garni, orange peel, potatoes and turmeric, and generous amounts of salt and pepper. Cover with water/stock.
Simmer until potatoes are cooked. Poach eggs in the soup and serve immediately.

Serves 6 *Miss Katrina Gruer, Edinburgh*

FISH

E NF COLD MACKEREL WITH BRETON SAUCE

4 even-sized mackerel
2 egg yolks
2 tablespoons french mustard
1 scant dessertspoon wine, cider or tarragon vinegar
2 tablespoons chopped Fresh herbs
salt, pepper
2 oz. butter, softened

Poach the mackerel, or wrap each fish in a piece of well oiled foil and bake in a moderate oven for 35-40 mins. The latter method of cooking keeps all the juices in and makes fish much easier to handle. Remove backbone of fish by opening it up flat and sliding finger under backbone, gently easing it from the flesh.

To make sauce blend the mustard with egg yolks and vinegar, add salt and pepper to taste. Soften butter until almost melted, taking care not to let it become oily, and gradually mix it into the sauce until it has the consistency of mayonnaise. Stir in chopped herbs. Parsley and chives are essential, and tarragon and chervil an ideal addition.

This sauce is quicker and easier to make than mayonnaise, and can be used with cold meat and poultry – and especially with pork.

45 mins
Serves 4 *Mrs Walter Steuart Fothringham, Dunkeld*

E F PILCHARD TRIANGLES

Short crust pastry
1 large tin pilchards
1 oz. fresh mushrooms
4 oz. grated cheese

Mash pilchards and add chopped mushrooms, 2 oz. grated cheese and seasoning.

Roll out pastry and cut into 8 squares, approx 6″ x 6″ each. Place a little of the mix in the centre of each and fold into triangles. Brush with milk or egg and sprinkle remaining cheese over top. Bake in moderate oven for approx. 30 mins. Delicious served cold with salad.

Serves 8 *Mrs M. Clacher, Pitlochry*

F TUNA OR PINK SALMON FISH CAKES

2 tins tuna or pink salmon
2 eggs
2 large onions
5 tablespoons medium motza meal or wholemeal flour
salt and pepper

Grate onions on large sized hole of a hand grater. Mix all ingredients together, and form into round flat rings about 1 inch in diameter and ¾ inch thick. Fry quickly in hot oil, which should only half cover the fish cake.
These quantities should make 24 fish cakes. Serve cold.

Mrs S. Abramsky, London

F SALMON MOUSSE

1½ lb. cooked salmon
1 breakfast cup mild mayonnaise
salt
cayenne pepper
lemon juice to taste
½ pint whipped cream
½ oz. gelatine dissolved in 1 tablespoon white wine and 1 tablespoon hot water

Mash salmon lightly with a fork, but do not liquidise. Mix thoroughly with mayonnaise. Season and add whipped cream, then gelatine. Transfer to dish in which it is to be served.
When quite cold, decorate with cucumber and aspic. If frozen, decorate after it has been defrosted.

20 mins
Serves 6-8 *The Hon. Mrs John Boyle, Dunkeld*

COLD SALMON

To cook salmon it is essential to have a decent-sized fish kettle, preferably one with a trivet.

Fill the fish kettle to about one inch above the trivet with $\frac{2}{3}$ water and $\frac{1}{3}$ white wine (cheap Spanish is the best). Take two small onions and stick each with 3 cloves, 2 carrots, 3 bay leaves, a dozen pepper corns, 3 large sprigs of parsley, a dessert-spoon of salt, and really anything else you fancy. I often use dried mixed vegetables with equal success. Boil everything hard for 1 hour. Meantime take a salmon, fresh or frozen, clean it and wash it well.

After the brew has boiled hard for 1 hour take the fish kettle off the heat and put in the salmon, back down or tummy side up (it should barely be in the liquid). Put the fish kettle back on the heat and simmer gently for 5 minutes. Take off heat and put in larder with the lid *on*. Leave until cold.

For some unknown reason the salmon is perfectly cooked irrespective of size.

This is an economical dish only if you have been given the salmon.

Anthony Dixon, Louth

E F

FRESH OR SMOKED HADDOCK CHOWDER (Cullen Skink)

- 3 lbs. fresh haddock or smoked haddock fillets
- 2 lbs. peeled and quartered potatoes
- 1 pint milk
- 3 large onions, chopped
- 6 slices bacon (smoked with fresh fish – green with smoked fish)
- salt, pepper

Fry bacon over very low heat until fat liquifies and bacon is crisp. Cook onions until soft, add potatoes and cover with 1 pint water. Place boned fish on top of potatoes and allow to steam gently. Simmer until potatoes are cooked and soft, add 1 pint milk. Mash potatoes and fish coarsely with a fork. Add tablespoon butter and adjust seasoning with salt and pepper. Serve with cream crackers.

The haddock chowder was made after a day's fishing. A big pot was put on the fire and the "stew" eaten by fishermen, out of half-pint mugs, after the catch had been gutted and stowed, as the boat chugged home.

30 mins

Serves 4-6

Mr Pierce (Maine fisherman) and Mr Bowie (Buckie fisherman)

Very traditional recipe in all fishing communities on both sides of the Atlantic

Mrs R. T. A. Ross, Pitlochry

♔ NF SCAMPI AU VIN DES ILES

Gently cook scampi in a heavy pan in a little butter, reducing the juice of the scampi for about 15 minutes. Then flamber in Bristol Milk Sherry to obtain a degree of caramelisation, though not too much. Add cream, turning the pan by hand to avoid curdling. Reduce again until the mixture is a smooth consistency. Serve with oriental rice only.

25 mins
Cook as many scampi as required

Max Nano, Grand Chef and late Maitre d'hotel of the Kensington Palace Hotel

Sir Alexander Glen, Stanton, Broadway

E FISH WITH CRISP CHEESE TOPPING

- 4 fillets white fish (haddock or whiting)
- 4 oz. marg
- 4 oz. grated cheese (mild Cheddar, Wensleydale, or Cheshire)
- 1 tablespoon flour
- 1 level teaspoon mustard powder
- salt, pepper

Cream all ingredients for the topping together. Spread over fish and bake in hot oven for 15-20 mins, until cheese mixture is crisp. If necessary finish under grill.

This has proved popular both with children and at informal dinner parties.

10 mins
Serves 4

Mrs E. F. Aglen, Ballintuim

E KEDGEREE

- 8 oz. cooked fish (preferably Arbroath smokies, this being my place of birth)
- 4 oz. cooked rice
- 2 oz. butter
- 2 hard-boiled eggs
- chopped parsley
- salt and cayenne pepper

Flake fish and mix with cooked rice. Melt the butter, add rice and fish mixture and stir over gentle heat until thoroughly hot. Season and add chopped white of egg. Heap up on a hot dish and garnish with sieved egg yolk and chopped parsley.

Old family recipe

30 mins
Serves 4

Douglas Crawford, M.P. for Perth & East Perthshire, House of Commons

E NF TROUT IN SHERRY SAUCE

2 x 1 lb. or 1 x 2 lb. trout
1 cup of thin cream
1 glass of sherry
2 oz. butter
flour
salt and pepper

Melt butter in a large flat fireproof dish in a hot oven (400°). Dust the cleaned trout in seasoned flour and dip in melted butter, turn it, return dish to oven till nicely brown (5-10 mins). Remove dish from oven and add cup of thin cream or top of milk and one wineglass of sherry. Baste well. Reduce oven heat to 300° and cook for 20 mins or longer if fish is large.
Baste well with juices and garnish with parsley. This is a delicious main course served with new potatoes and peas, but is not suitable for small trout. *This is an economical dish if you've caught the trout yourself.*

40 mins

Mary Robb, who was for many years cook to Col. and Mrs Don of Glenshee

Serves 4-5

Mrs Cecil Howman, Dunkeld

E F BROWN TROUT PIE

2 lbs. brown trout
4 hard-boiled eggs, chopped
2 oz. flour
2 oz. butter
breadcrumbs, dried
seasoning

Clean trout, poach gently including the heads, in salted water. When cooked remove meat from bones, keeping liquid in which they were cooked. Melt flour and butter together, adding enough fish stock to make a sauce. Simmer a few minutes, add seasoning to taste.
Add fish and eggs, mix and place in ovenproof dish. Cover with breadcrumbs, dot with butter and brown in oven or under the grill.

30 mins
Serves 4

Own invention
Mrs Ronald Thorburn, Enochdhu

KILTY POTATOES

Cut raw potatoes into fine needles and put a layer of these into a well buttered fireproof dish. Follow this with a layer of filleted kippers, then another layer of potatoes.
Pour thick cream over the top. Place dish in a hot oven for ½-¾ of an hour.

Mrs R. S. Stewart-Wilson, Tulliemet

FUINE BREAC
(Baked trout, traditional Scottish style)

Take 4 gutted fresh trout and place in a buttered dish. Sprinkle with finely sliced onions and chopped garlic. Sprinkle 1 oz. per fish of pinhead oatmeal on to trout, add 2 cups dry white wine. Cover dish and bake in oven at gas mark 4 or 5 for 20 mins.

Serves 4 *Lawrence Healy, Chef, Pitlochry Hydro Hotel*

POACHED TAY TROUT, STUFFED WITH MUSHROOM PATE

Take 4 good-sized gutted fresh trout, stuff with mushroom pâté and cook in a stock of wine, oil or butter, water, black pepper-corns, parsley and sliced onion. Simmer for 5-7 mins. Serve cold with finely-chopped cucumber and yoghurt, flavoured with lime or lemon juice.

Mushroom pâté filling (this can be frozen):

- 2 oz. fresh unsalted butter
- 1 lb. minced button mushrooms
- 1 pint rough red wine
- 4 oz. onions, minced
- seasoning

Melt butter in thick pan over slow heat. Add onions and cook gently for 5 mins. Add mushrooms and seasoning and stir together. Add wine and leave to simmer for 1½ hours until mixture is dry.

This is a real favourite with our foreign guests.

Serves 4 *Lawrence Healy, Chef, Pitlochry Hydro Hotel*

E HERRING AND APPLE CASSEROLE

- 2 lbs. fresh herrings, filleted
- 2 teaspoons salt
- 2 tablespoons butter
- 2 medium onions, finely chopped
- 4 tart apples, grated or sliced
- 2 tablespoons breadcrumbs
- 2 tablespoons grated cheese

Sprinkle herrings with salt. Fry onion in butter (with the herring roe, if any). Cover bottom of large shallow baking dish (buttered) with apples, sprinkle onion over, and place herring over with skin side up. Sprinkle with breadcrumbs and grated cheese, dot with butter.
Bake for 15-20 mins in hot oven (475°) and serve hot with mashed potatoes.

25 mins
Serves 4-6

Norwegian recipe
Mrs M. Collins, Rannoch

E NF HADDOCK WITH ORANGE

- 6 pieces haddock fillet
- 6 slices brown or white bread made into breadcrumbs
- ½ grated orange
- juice of 2 medium oranges
- 3 oz. butter
- 1 clove crushed garlic
- salt, pepper

Grease a large ovenproof dish with butter. Roll haddock into log shape and place in dish, season. Melt remaining butter in frying pan, add garlic and cook for 1 min. Add breadcrumbs and grated orange. Stir till all butter is absorbed.
Cover dish with breadcrumb mixture and orange juice. Dot with extra butter or margarine. Bake uncovered in oven at 375° or gas mark 5 for 30-40 mins. *This dish is excellent with salads.*

15 mins
Serves 4-5

Own recipe of Spanish origin
Mrs Peter Barr, Tenandry

HOT HADDOCK MOUSSE

2 oz. butter
2 oz. flour
3 eggs
1 cup milk
1 haddock, smoked

Put 2 oz. butter and 2 oz. flour into saucepan. Add 1 cup milk by degrees, bring to the boil and allow to cook, adding a little pepper. Lightly grill the haddock, chop and add to the mixture. Add 3 yolks of eggs and beat it up. Whip the whites to a stiff froth and mix all together.
Put into soufflé dish and steam for ¾ hour. To serve turn out and pour a mushroom sauce over.

Serves 4 *Mrs R. S. Stewart-Wilson, Tulliemet*

F TROUT WITH NUTS

trout
flour, salt and pepper
1½ oz. butter for each trout
½ oz. almonds (flaked) or salted peanuts for each fish
squeeze of lemon

Clean and wash the trout, leaving the head on, and coat with seasoned flour. Melt butter in frying pan. Fry fish on both sides until golden (12 mins). In smaller pan melt some butter and fry nuts until pale brown. Squeeze lemon on to nuts and pour over fish on hot serving dish.
Serve with wedges of lemon, green salad, garden peas and new potatoes.

30 mins

Mrs Kenneth MacVicar, Kenmore

GOLDEN SAVOURY

Mix 1 breakfastcup flaked fish (cooked) with ¼ pint white sauce, 1 tablespoon chopped parsley, ½ teaspoon dry mustard, and pour into pie dish. Heat a cupful of mashed potatoes with 1 oz. marg and 1 tablespoon milk and beat till fluffy. Add pepper and salt and beat in 1 egg yolk. Lastly fold in very gently stiffly beaten egg white.

Put carefully on top of fish and sprinkle with 1 tablespoon grated cheese. Bake in hot oven for 15-20 mins till well risen and nicely brown.

Mrs M. W. G. Robertson, Pitlochry

E F HADDOCK AND TOMATO SERVED ON A NEST OF RICE

- 1 lb. smoked haddock
- medium sized tin peeled tomatoes or ¾ lb. fresh tomatoes
- 2 teaspoons finely chopped shallot or onion
- 2 oz. butter or marg
- 2 tablespoons flour
- 1 cup milk
- salt, pepper
- chopped parsley

Poach haddock in milk. Make sauce by frying the onions in butter till lightly coloured, add flour and cook to a smooth paste. Using the milk in which fish was cooked, make sauce. Season, add chopped tomatoes, continue cooking. Finally add flaked haddock and reheat.

Wash 8 oz. rice, half fill pan of fast boiling salted water and throw in rice. Boil for 12 to 15 mins till tender. Strain at once, pour cold water over. Dry rice in cool oven or shake over a low gas over and over again. Serve fish on bed of rice for a luncheon or supper dish.

30 mins — Recipe learned at Mrs Black's cookery school, Glasgow, over 80 years ago by mother

Serves 4 — *Miss M. D. Finnie, Pitlochry*

NF A WAY WITH CURRIED PRAWNS

Brown a couple of sliced onions in butter. Add whatever you have lying about – a tomato, a bit of chicken, a few mushrooms. Add a couple of teaspoons of curry powder (curry powders vary enormously and you have to learn your own powder and your own taste). Simmer for at least 10 minutes, but really the longer the better. If short you have a kind of curry broth – if long you have a thick brown sauce.

When ready to eat – which means about 12 minutes after you've started boiling your rice – bung in the prawns, stir only once and very gently. When uniformly hot, serve.

Rice was, in my youth, popularly regarded as difficult. Not so. Boil a good deal of water with a pinch of salt. Add the rice. After about ten minutes brisk boiling, take a fork and taste. When you feel your teeth going through the grains, but they're not hard, pour off water, add a pat of butter and dry for a couple of minutes, tossing with the fork.

Make a ring of rice on the plate and put the prawns in the middle.

15 mins
Serves 2 or 3 *Ronald Mavor, Edinburgh*

E NF LEMON BAKED HADDOCK

6 pieces filleted haddock	2 bay leaves
2 large lemons	salt, pepper

Fold fish in half lengthways, dust the fillets with salt and pepper. Slice the lemons thinly, cover fillets with slices of lemon and tuck the bay leaves between them. Bake the fish in a moderate oven, 355° or gas mark 4, for 15-20 mins.

This is one of the simplest and most delicious ways to cook any white fish, but one has to be very careful not to overcook it.

5 mins
Serves 4-5 *Mrs A. Cunningham, Rannoch*

MEAT, GAME & POULTRY

NF ENTRECOTE MARCHAND DE VIN
"Winemerchant's Steak"

Fry in butter two seasoned entrecôte steaks (sirloin), using a heavy frying pan, until underdone or well done according to taste. Remove to a dish, top each with a little bone marrow if available, and keep warm while sauce is made.

Add more butter to pan, with a chopped shallot and 3 or 4 mushrooms, also chopped. Sauter gently, add a wineglass of red wine, one teaspoon tomato purée, pepper and salt. Simmer slowly for 5-6 mins until syrupy. Pour over the steaks and sprinkle with chopped parsley.

This is for people who do not like a dry steak. Marrow is not really necessary, but shallot is better than onion. Before the 1939/45 war there was a small but distinguished restaurant in Soho called Le Rendezvous. So popular was its cooking that its owner published a little book of complete menus, all simply made versions of the classic French cuisine. My mother and grandmother (the latter wrote the Daily Telegraph cookery articles under the name "A country housewife" from 1936 to 1939) were keen collectors of recipes. I found this in typescript taken from the Rendezvous cookery book, but the wording has been changed.

15 mins — Classic French recipe

Serves 2 — *Lady Balfour of Burleigh, Brucefield, Clackmannan*

E NF GOULASH FROM VIENNA

- 2 lb. shin of beef
- 2 lb. onions
- 12 small Viennese sausages
- 1 level teaspoon caraway seed
- 1 level teaspoon marjoram
- pepper, salt
- 12 small potatoes or 6 medium potatoes
- 12 small gherkins
- 3 dessertspoons (heaped) paprika
- oil

Put 2 dessertspoons oil into heavy pan. Chop onions and cook in oil until golden and very soft. Stir frequently (this takes an hour). Chop meat into 2″ pieces and brown meat in onions. Add marjoram, caraway seed, salt and pepper, and about ½ pint stock. Add 12 small gherkins. Simmer on *very* low heat for 3 or 4 hours.

When ready for meal add sausages, pre-cooked potatoes and paprika. Cook together for 30 mins. Serve with salad and red wine.

Note: it is most important not to put paprika in until the final 30 mins. This dish is even better if kept for a day or even 2 days, and then heated through.

This recipe, over 100 *years old, was given to me by Count Poldi Lamare, a wonderful Viennese designer for the theatre and a superb cook. I asked him to teach me how to make this dish, and he arrived on my doorstep at* 7.30 *in the morning and made me start at once to cook under his orders. This is now a must for my guests, because the slaving over the stove can be suffered in advance and it is possible to look cool and collected when they arrive.*

1½ hours
Serves 6 *Miss Joan Kemp Welch, London*

E F ALLIGATOR STEW

1 lb. minced steak
2 medium-sized onions
1 15 oz. tin baked beans in tomato sauce
salt, pepper

Put a layer of roughly broken up lumps of mince in the bottom of an ovenproof casserole. Add a layer of sliced onions and season well. Continue to add layers of mince and onions and seasoning, and finally pour over the tin of baked beans, rinsing out the tin with a little water.

Cook in a slow oven (300°) for about an hour and a half. Stir well after about half an hour. Serve with mashed potatoes and coleslaw.

10 mins
Serves 4-5 *Mrs George Crerar, Pitlochry*

E F BEEF CURRY

3 lbs. stewing steak, cubed
2 onions, sliced
2 cloves garlic, crushed
3 dessertspoons curry powder, mild or hot
2 bay leaves
lemon juice
brown sugar
$\frac{1}{2}$ pint stock
beef dripping
salt

1. Toss meat cubes in the curry powder and salt and leave covered overnight.
2. Using a heavy cast-iron casserole fry onions and garlic gently in dripping.
3. Add meat and fry at least 2-3 mins, stirring all the time.
4. Add stock and bay leaves, simmer for 2 hours.
5. Towards end of cooking time check seasoning and add a squeeze of lemon juice and spoonful of brown sugar. More curry powder may be added if gently fried first.
6. Allow to cool and stand for at least 24 hours before reheating and serving with plain boiled rice, and side dishes of chutney, pickles, poppadums, banana, etc.

This curry is semi-dry but very succulent if good quality steak is used. If freezing, remember to let it stand for 24 hours before freezing to allow good flavour to develop.

2 days altogether — Indian recipe
Serves 8 — *Mrs Hubert Strathairn, Crieff*

E YOGHURT KHORESHE

$1\frac{1}{2}$ lbs. mince
1 teaspoon salt
$\frac{1}{2}$ teaspoon black pepper
$\frac{1}{2}$ teaspoon turmeric
2 tablespoons butter or marg
2 tablespoons oil
1 finely chopped onion

Sauce:

2 teaspoons curry powder
6 cloves, crushed
1 teaspoon ground cardamon
1 cup hot water
1 cup plain yoghurt
$\frac{1}{4}$ cup chopped parsley

Mix mince, salt, pepper and turmeric. Form into small 1″ balls. Heat butter and oil in pan and brown meat balls on all sides. Transfer to flame-proof casserole. Cook onion in pan till transparent and put in casserole.
Mix curry powder, cloves and cardamon, sprinkle over casserole. Add hot water, stirring carefully. Bring to boil, cover and simmer 35 mins. Skim off fat, stir in yoghurt, reheat but do not boil. Sprinkle parsley on Khoreshe and serve.
The meat balls will freeze. Sauce should be made fresh.

15 mins
Serves 6 hungry people

Persian recipe
Over a thousand years old
Mrs R. S. Barbour, Fincastle

E F POST PARTY BEEF

2 lbs. braising beef
1 large onion
$\frac{1}{2}$ bottle stout
Worcester sauce or mushroom ketchup
$\frac{1}{4}$ lb. mushrooms

Dust beef with seasoned flour and place in lidded ovenware dish. Slice onion thinly and spread on top of beef. Arrange mushrooms round, pour over stout, sauce or ketchup. Cover with double greaseproof paper and then the lid. Cook in slow oven (300°) for 3-4 hours. It will not spoil by long cooking. Can of course be made with smaller quantities.
This recipe was evolved to cope with a meal for a houseful of guests after a cocktail party, thus avoiding trying to cook after a few drinks in party clothes and high-heeled shoes. It never fails.

10 mins
Serves 6-8

Mrs Cecil Howman, Dunkeld

E F SHERRIED HAMBURGER CASSEROLE

6 rashers bacon
1 medium onion, sliced
1 clove garlic, minced (optional)
3 tablespoons fine dry crumbs
1 lb. minced beef
1 beaten egg
½ teaspoon salt
pepper to taste
½ teaspoon mixed herbs
4 oz. mushrooms
tin of cream of mushroom soup
2 tablespoons sherry or wine

Cut bacon into strips after removing rind, fry until crisp. Remove and drain. Fry onion and garlic over low heat till tender, add crumbs, mix well and cook a few minutes longer. Mix with beef, egg and seasonings. Shape into 12 balls or flat cakes on a floured board, brown well in bacon fat and put into casserole. Fry mushrooms lightly after slicing them, mix with mushroom soup and the sherry or wine and add to mixture already in casserole. Sprinkle with fried pieces of bacon over top of casserole. Cover and bake in moderate oven, 380° or gas mark 5, for about 45 mins. *Do not freeze sauce. This can be added when the dish is needed.*

20 mins
Serves 5-6

Mrs M. Riddell, Glenlyon

NF FILLET OF BEEF IN MADEIRA WITH PATE SAUCE

Pre-heat oven to 475°, gas mark 9, and slightly salt a 2½lb. fillet of beef. Cut a slit lengthways down the side of the beef and stuff with ½ lb. streaky bacon. Put small dots of lard all over beef, melt ¼ lb. butter and pour over. Cook for 5 mins, baste well, adding 1 teacup of Madeira to juices. Cook for 25 mins altogether for medium rare meat.

Pâté sauce: Use 8 oz. coarse pâté to which 2 tablespoons double cream and some of the juice from the cooked meat should be added. *This makes a sauce of thick paste consistency.*

30 mins
Serves 6 *Mrs R. Adams, Dalnaspidal*

F

MEAT LOAF

1 egg, slightly beaten
2 teaspoons salt
$\frac{3}{4}$ cup water or milk
1 cup soft breadcrumbs
strips of bacon
2 tablespoons minced onion (or dried onion)
2 lb. minced beef
good pinch mixed herbs or rosemary

Mix together all the above ingredients. Put into greased loaf tin and lay some strips of bacon on top. Bake for about 1 hour at 350°. Serve hot with warmed tomato sauce, or cold with salad and chutney or relish.
This is a basic recipe and can be varied in many ways.

15 mins American recipe
Serves 6 *Mrs Lawson, Castlebeigh Hotel, Pitlochry*

MEAT ROLL

1 lb. steak, minced
$\frac{1}{2}$ lb. Belfast ham
$\frac{1}{4}$ lb. sausage meat
1 cup porridge oats
$1\frac{1}{2}$ cup liquid, stock or water
1 egg to bind

Combine all the above ingredients.
Bake in 2 loaf tins at gas mark 4 for $1\frac{1}{4}$ hours.

Miss F. Mackinnon, Pitlochry

E MOUSSAKA OF BEEF

- 1 lb. lean minced beef
- 3 fl. oz. salad oil
- 3 medium onions, chopped
- 1 tablespoon parsley, minced
- 4 tablespoons water
- 1 tablespoon tomato purée
- 2 teaspoons salt
- 4 oz. Parmesan cheese
- ½ teaspoon freshly ground black pepper
- 1 tin ratatouille or equivalent amount of home-made
- 2 egg whites, well beaten
- 1½ oz. bread or cornflake crumbs
- ½ pint medium white sauce

Heat oil in heavy frying pan and brown meat lightly. Add onions, parsley, water, tomato purée, salt and pepper. Simmer over low heat for about 25 mins, stirring occasionally. Add egg whites and crumbs to the meat mixture and blend until they are absorbed.

In a medium casserole make alternate layers of ratatouille and meat mixture, ending with ratatouille. Pour on the white sauce (made with 1 oz. butter or marg, 1 oz. flour, ½ pint milk and seasoning) and sprinkle the cheese over the top.

Bake in medium oven at about 350° for 30 mins or until well browned.

45 mins

Serves up to 6 *Mrs D. Misselbrook, Aberfeldy*

E F FLANAGAN SPECIAL

- 1 lb. minced steak
- 1 tin oxtail soup (medium, condensed)
- 1 large onion
- salt, pepper
- fat for frying

Chop onion and fry in fat until transparent. Place half the onions in greased casserole. Put half the meat on top and season. Spread half the soup over meat. Then repeat these three layers. Cheese can be sprinkled on top. Cover, bake in moderate oven for 1 hour. Serve hot with creamed potatoes and peas.

15 mins

Serves 4-6 *Mrs D. Menzies, Kenmore*

E SOVEREIGN ROAST

4 lb. piece of beef, topside or other pot roast joint
2 oz. butter
2 large onions
¾ pint stock
1 level dessertspoon syrup
2 level tablespoons white vinegar
3 tablespoons flour
1 tablespoon crushed peppercorns

Heat butter in a heavy casserole and brown the joint well. Remove joint and gently fry onions, add flour and lightly cook roux. Add stock, vinegar and syrup, stir until smooth over low heat.

Remove from heat, replace joint, add peppercorns tied in muslin. Cover with well-fitting lid or foil and cook for 3 *hours* or a little longer.

Other vegetables can be added during cooking, e.g. carrot, turnip. Good on a cold winter's day.

15 mins
Serves 6

Mrs J. D. Caldwell, Kinloch Rannoch

E F CASSOULET

¾ lb. haricot beans, ¾ lb. red kidney beans, soaked overnight and cooked till nearly tender
1 Mattessons smoked pork sausage, skinned
1 x 8 oz. tin hot dog sausages
2 sticks celery, sliced
2 carrots, sliced
1 x 2 lb. can tomatoes
herbs to taste, e.g. garlic salt, celery salt, paprika, oregano

Using a heavy cast iron casserole put layers of mixed beans, sliced sausages and vegetables into it. Add herbs and pour over tin of tomatoes. Bring to boil and simmer for approx. 1 hour.

20 mins
Serves 4

Mrs C. W. Grant, Pitlochry

CASSEROLE OF OXTAIL

1 oxtail
6 young carrots
1 large onion
1 tablespoon flour
seasoning

Cut the oxtail into sections, remove excess suet and fat. Put a little cooking oil on the bottom of casserole, heat this and fry oxtail pieces gently in it, turning them over to brown on all sides. Sprinkle in a heaped tablespoon plain flour and continue to fry for a few minutes. Add boiling water slowly to cover the pieces of oxtail. Season with salt and pepper and simmer slowly, either on top of the cooker or in the oven (325°) for 3 hours. Then add the diced carrot and onion. Top up liquid if necessary with boiling water and simmer for a further hour. Remove the pan from the heat and set in a cold place to allow fat to rise and solidify. Skim off fat, reheat gently and serve with potatoes and green vegetables. It is more convenient to prepare this dish the preceding day and allow the fat to solidify overnight, as it can then be easily and thoroughly removed. The most important point is thorough cooking to ensure that the meat comes easily away from the bone.

It is a true saying that the meat nearest the bone is the sweetest, and there is no meat which comes nearer the bone than that of an oxtail. This makes a very tasty dish.

Norman Renfrew, Provost, Perth & Kinross District Council, Perth

---

E F MARJORIE'S SMOKED OR SPICED BEEF

5-8 lb. brisket, trimmed, boned and rolled
3 cloves garlic
2 teaspoons saltpetre
3 tablespoons salt
5 tablespoons castor sugar
¼ teaspoon cinnamon
4 cloves garlic
5 tablespoons mixed pickling spices

Rub outside of meat with 3 cloves garlic and knife it into the meat. Rub dry ingredients all over the meat. Roll up into greaseproof paper and then wrap in foil and heavy brown paper. Leave in fridge for 14 days.

On the 15th day cook for 6-7 hours at 300/350°. Place in ½″ water for 4 hours. Cover the meat for the last 2 hours. Cool and slice finely. *Very good, slightly warmed, on rye bread.*

Mrs J. G. Fenton, Huntingtower

NF

ESCALOPE OF VEAL "SARAH ANNE"

- 2 good sprigs fresh tarragon, finely chopped
- 2 ripe avocados
- fresh garlic
- squeeze lemon juice
- black pepper
- touch of olive oil
- seasoning
- 2 oz. unsalted butter
- 1 tablespoon olive oil
- 6 escalopes of veal, well flattened
- ¼ pint double cream
- good tot Bénédictine

Set oven at 275°. Skin, stone and dice avocados, beat to a pulp with garlic to taste, a pinch of salt, ground black pepper, a squeeze of lemon juice and the touch of olive oil. Transfer to ovenproof dish and cover with buttered paper or foil. Finely chop tarragon, flatten veal to at least the size of a side plate. Place avocado mixture in oven. Heat oil and butter in heavy frying pan until foam subsides. Cook escalopes over moderate heat – usually pan size will only allow one at a time, and it should not take more than a minute or so for each side. *Do not overcook*. Keep warm in oven while cooking the other escalopes. Replace meat in pan, with any juices that may have gathered on plate in oven. Quickly flamber with Bénédictine over a hot flame, and when flame goes out remove meat, and wrap each escalope round some of the avocado mixture to form a kind of sandwich. Keep warm. Return pan with juices to flame, add cream and tarragon. Boil until reduced, taking care not to separate the cream.

Check seasoning when sauce is thick, pour over meat and avocado and serve at once.
Note: *Veal must be well trimmed to avoid shrinkage or curling during cooking. To help flatten the escalopes use a moistened plastic bag to avoid meat sticking to the bat. Never flamber straight from the bottle. I have witnessed a very nasty accident when a bottle blew up in our chef's hand. A great waste of liquor!*

30 mins — *Andrew Mackenzie, Loch Tummel*
Serves 6 — *Hotel, Strathtummel*

E COTE DE VEAU A LA SASSI

4 veal cutlets	butter
flour	sherry
seasoning	fresh sage

Flour and season meat. Cook in butter till golden brown on each side and keep hot in oven. Add a glass of sherry to the pan and 6-10 leaves of fresh sage. Reduce for 2 mins and pour over meat. Serve immediately.
Beaten pork fillets do just as well and are cheaper.

20 mins
Serves 4 — *Lady Keith, Strathtummel*

VEAL WITH TOMATOES AND CREAM

Beat escalopes of veal well, sizzle quickly in butter, with some chopped tomatoes, until just cooked. Pour in some fresh cream but do *not* allow it to boil.
Stir up all the delicious juices, season well, remove tomato skins and serve with boiled rice.
This looks and tastes delicious and really can be produced in about 10 mins with the greatest of ease.

10 mins

Mrs A. M. Robertson, Dunkeld

E F MUTTON CASSEROLE WITH LEMON

4 round mutton chops
1 onion
1 carrot
1 tablespoon tomato purée
1 green pepper
1 lemon

Lightly fry chopped onion and brown chops on both sides. Place onion in bottom of casserole (for oven cooking) or heavy pan (for top of stove), place chops on top, cover with sliced pepper, carrot cut into thin fingers, and grated rind of lemon. Add half pint stock or gravy, to which has been added one tablespoon tomato purée and juice of lemon.
Cover and cook for 1½ hours in slow oven (300°), or 1 hour on top of stove on slow heat. Serve with green vegetables and boiled potatoes.

15 mins
Serves 4

Mrs Tom Finlayson, Aberfeldy

E CHINESE QUICKIE

½ lb. lean lamb
1 tablespoon cornflour
2 teaspoons sugar
1 tablespoon soy sauce
2 tablespoons sherry – a little more if liked
8 stalks spring onions or chives, chopped fairly finely

Make a sauce of these ingredients, add the meat cut into paper thin slices about ¾ inch wide and 1½ inches long.
Fry in a little oil and butter for about 3 mins.

10 mins
Serves 4

The Misses Audrey and Jean Wright, Auchtibert Dunalastair

E F VICTORIAN LAMB

approx. 3 lb. roast shoulder of lamb

topping: 2 large onions
2 tablespoons butter
1 clove garlic, crushed
4 tablespoons white breadcrumbs
little stock to moisten

rind and juice of $\frac{1}{2}$ lemon
2 teaspoons rosemary
1 heaped teaspoon each of English, French and German mustard
salt and pepper to taste

Portion ready-cooked lamb and place on a heatproof flat dish. Fry finely chopped onion and garlic in butter until tender but not brown. Add mustards, lemon, and rest of ingredients. Mix well and spread over each portion of lamb. Grill slowly for 5 mins until crispy but not burnt.
Thicken gravy from previously cooked joint and serve with mashed piped potatoes, vegetables of your choice or grilled tomatoes.
This makes a delicious change with the left-overs of the Sunday joint, and is greatly appreciated by many of our guests.

20 mins
Serves 6

Mrs Turk, Fasganeon Hotel, Pitlochry

E F BOBOTI

1. Mince together 1 lb. cold mutton with 1 slice white bread soaked in milk with good sized onion which has been browned in oil or butter or a mixture of both.

2. Make a sauce of the following:
   - 1 tablespoon chutney
   - 1 tablespoon curry powder
   - 1 large tablespoon apricot jam
   - 2 teaspoons brown sugar
   - salt and pepper to taste
   - a very little vinegar

3. Mix nos. 1 and 2 together and put in greased ovenproof dish. Pour over a custard made with 1 egg and a little milk. Decorate with slices of lemon and blanched almonds and a few dots of butter. Bake in slow oven for 40 mins. Serve with rice and chutney.

40 mins
Serves 4

South African recipe
The Countess of Wemyss, Longniddry

E NF LENINGRAD LAMB

1½ lb. lamb cutlets
2 teaspoons cinnamon
2 oz. cooking fat
carton of natural yoghurt or sour cream
2 medium-sized onions
½ green pepper
packet gouda cheese slices
salt, black pepper

Sprinkle lamb with cinnamon, salt and black pepper, place in shallow ovenproof dish. Smear about ½ oz. of the fat on the top of the chops. Cover dish with foil and place in slow oven, 300°-325°, for 1½ hours.

Meanwhile chop onions and pepper, fry gently in remainder of the fat for a few minutes. After 1½ hours remove chops from oven. If gravy has become very fatty, some of the fat may be removed at this stage, before covering the chops with the onion and pepper, and the cheese slices.

Return uncovered to hot oven, 400°, for further 20 mins. Just before serving add the yoghurt, stirring it in without disturbing the cheese crust. Return to oven once again for 2-3 mins. This is particularly delicious served with jacket potatoes and green vegetables. *This recipe is particularly economical if made with neck of New Zealand lamb.*

30 mins
Serves 4

Lady Alexander, Callender

E F PORK CHOPS IN CIDER

6 pork chops
2 green peppers
2 onions
¼ pint cider

Wipe and trim chops, dip in seasoned flour. Sauter quickly in 2 oz. butter or marg. Transfer to ovenproof dish, greased, adding sliced onions and de-seeded and sliced peppers. Add more salt and pepper, then cider.

Cook slowly for 2 hours in moderate oven. Serve with mashed potatoes and any vegetable available.

Holme Rose cook

15 mins
Serves 6

The Rt. Hon. Lord Campbell of Croy, M.C., Cawdor

E NF CRUNCHY-TOPPED GRILLED PORK CHOPS

Grill 4 pork chops, seasoned with salt and pepper and brushed with melted butter.

About 5 mins before they are ready, spread one side with a mixture of:

2 level teaspoons dry mustard
4 level teaspoons demerara sugar
1 oz. chopped salted peanuts
½ teaspoon Worcester sauce
1 teaspoon vinegar
½ level teaspoon salt
1 teaspoon melted butter

Return to grill and cook until golden brown. Serve with cored apple rings which have been lightly fried on both sides in a little butter.

20 mins
Serves 4

Mrs F. Carruthers, Moulin

E POLYNESIAN PORK CHOPS

2 large or 4 small pork chops
garlic (optional)
salt
pepper

Sauce:

2 x 4½ oz. tins (1 cup) strained fruit dessert (baby food tins)
⅓ cup tomato ketchup
⅓ cup vinegar
½ cup brown sugar
2 level teaspoons ground ginger
2 dessertspoons soy sauce
1 level teaspoon salt

Season chops with garlic, salt and pepper. Brown in a shallow pan and spoon off fat. Place chops in fireproof oven dish. Mix all sauce ingredients together. Pour over chops, cook for a further 40-45 mins at 350° or gas mark 5, or until meat is cooked. Serve on bed of cooked long grain rice, with peas and sweet corn.

15 mins

Serves 2-4

Mrs A. W. Bates, Moulin

E F PORK IN ORANGE SAUCE

6 large pork fillets or 8 small
1 small tin peeled tomatoes
1 orange
1 onion
stock cube
1½ tablespoons flour
brown sugar
white wine

Trim fat from fillets and brown in butter with a little olive oil, remove to casserole dish. Add peeled and chopped onion to fat and cook till soft. Make a roux with flour and white wine, add stock to gravy thickness. Add tomatoes and pour over fillets. Cover and cook at 355° or gas mark 4 for 1 hour. Put juice and rind of orange in pan with 1 tablespoon brown sugar till melted. Half an hour before serving pour over meat and continue cooking *uncovered.*

Serves 4

Mrs Charles Tennant, Blairgowrie

PORK STROGANOFF

- 1 lb. pork fillet or tenderloin
- 1 oz. butter
- 1 tablespoon oil
- 4 oz. lean streaky bacon rashers, rinded
- ½ lb. mushrooms, sliced
- ½ lb. tomatoes, peeled and chopped, or 1 tin tomatoes
- 1 x 5 fl. oz. carton sour cream
- ¼ pint strong chicken stock

Cut pork into strips. Coat well in flour. Heat butter and oil in frying pan, add meat and fry until brown all over. Put meat to one side and keep warm. Scissor snip bacon into strips, add to pan, fry until brown. Put aside with meat. Cook mushrooms in same pan until tender and add tomatoes. Return pork and bacon to pan, stir well, add cream and stock. Loosen residue from pan base, bring to boil, check seasoning. Reduce heat and simmer for about 20 mins., stirring occasionally.

Serve with diced fried potatoes and leaf spinach. *This is a good lunch party dish.*

30 mins
Serves 4

Mrs T. Rossaak, Johannesburg

E NF CELEBRATION GAMMON

- ½ a Danish gammon (about 8 lbs) smoked or unsmoked
- 2 tablespoons made-up mustard
- 2 tablespoons soft brown sugar
- maraschino or glacé cherries
- cloves or cocktail sticks

Heat oven to 400° or gas mark 6. Weigh gammon, wrap in foil, place in large roasting tin half filled with water. Allow 25 mins per lb. Cook until 25 mins before end of cooking time.

Blend mustard and sugar. Remove rind from gammon and brush fat with the mixture. Cook for the remaining 25 mins until just browning. Halve cherries and arrange over gammon, using cloves or cocktail sticks to anchor them. Serve gammon hot or cold.

Mrs Colin Horsfall, Leamington Spa

NF HAWAIIAN GAMMON

4 slices gammon, 1 inch thick
small can pineapple slices
4 cloves
oil

Sauce:

12 glacé cherries
mint leaves, parsley
1 level teaspoon dry mustard
1 level teaspoon cornflour
1 tablespoon water

1. Trim rind from gammon.
2. Arrange four slices pineapple on top.
3. Spike gammon fat with cloves, and brush with oil.
4. Place in ovenproof dish. Pour over pineapple juice from can.
5. Bake 20-30 mins in moderately hot oven (400° or gas mark 5).
6. When cooked remove cloves and put gammon and pineapple on serving dish. Decorate with cherries and mint leaves, garnish with parsley.

Sauce:

1. Mix mustard and cornflour to paste with 1 tablespoon water.
2. Add juice from oven dish.
3. Cook for 3 mins on top of cooker, season if liked.

Serves 4 30 mins *Marjory Lady Bonar, Pitlochry*

NF JAMBON A LA CREME

6 shallots
4 tablespoons butter
4 tablespoons flour
¾ cup milk
¾ cup cream
6-8 thin slices ham
¼ cup dry white wine
2 tablespoons tomato purée

Chop shallots finely and cook in butter, but do not brown. Add flour, stir into a paste, then gradually stir in milk and cream and allow it to thicken, stirring constantly. Add purée and wine and let it blend well. Simmer over hot water for 25-30 mins but it must not boil.

Heat ham, cut into strips. Arrange on serving dish, cover with sauce, glaze under grill before serving.

30 mins
Serves 6-8

French recipe
Mrs Barbara Liddell, Pitlochry

CHICKEN SALAD IN CURRIED RING

E F

1 cooked chicken
1 pint chicken stock
½ oz. gelatine
1 tablespoon curry powder
1 small onion, grated
4 hard-boiled eggs
1 teacup mayonnaise
salt, pepper
1 tablespoon lemon juice
blanched almonds

Melt gelatine in stock, chop eggs and add with curry powder and mayonnaise to gelatine mixture. *Keep stirring* till set. Pour into ring and put in fridge.
Chop up chicken, add 1 tablespoon lemon juice, grated onion and blanched chopped almonds. Fill curried ring with chicken and serve with tossed salad.

30 mins
Serves 6-8 *Miss Mary Douglas, Ballinluig*

CHICKEN SALAD WITH AVOCADO AND GREENS

¾ pint mayonnaise
6 oz. seedless raisins, soaked in white wine, drained
4 oz. salted peanuts
½ pint mango chutney, cut into slivers
4 oz. flaked coconut
lemon juice
2 lb. cooked chicken, cut in slivers
2 cups bananas, diagonally sliced
salt and pepper to taste
salad greens
additional sliced bananas
avocado slices

Mix together mayonnaise, raisins, peanuts, chutney and coconut. Toss with chicken meat. Gently combine with bananas, season with salt and pepper. Mound in a large dish with lettuce. Garnish chicken mixture with slices of banana and avocado, which have been dipped in lemon juice.
I have found this unusual salad much admired. It is suitable for buffet lunches or rather special picnic parties.

Serves 12 30 mins *Lady Fraser, Bankfoot*

E F SWEDISH CHICKEN SALAD

- $3\frac{1}{2}$ lb. roasted chicken – cold, or
- $3\frac{1}{2}$ lb. boiled fowl – cold
- 6 oz. Patna rice
- 1 green apple
- 2 bananas
- lemon juice
- $\frac{1}{4}$ pint double cream
- $\frac{1}{3}$ pint mayonnaise
- 1 level teaspoon curry powder
- salt and pepper
- watercress for garnish

1. Carve cold chicken or fowl and cut into 1-inch strips. Cook rice and cool.
2. Core and thinly slice apple, leaving skin on. Peel and thickly slice bananas. Dredge both with lemon juice. A Jiffy lemon may be used.
3. Whip cream until same consistency as mayonnaise, and combine the two.
4. Add curry powder. Fold in chicken, apple and bananas. Add more lemon juice and adjust seasoning.

Serve with lettuce salad.

The chicken, rice and mayonnaise mixture can be prepared well in advance, but must be mixed together shortly before the meal. This only takes a few minutes.

Swedish recipe

Serves 6 *Mrs M. Mackenzie Smith, Blairgowrie*

E NF POULET A LA CREME

- roasting chicken
- $\frac{1}{2}$ pint approx. double or whipping cream
- $\frac{1}{2}$ lb. white grapes
- Harvey's sauce
- Worcester sauce
- seasoning

Roast chicken, remove flesh from bones and place in a fireproof dish. Slightly whip cream, add sauces and seasoning to taste. Pour over chicken, heat thoroughly and serve.

Peel the grapes and put over dish just before serving.

20 mins *Nicholas Fairbairn, Q.C., M.P.,*
Serves 4 *House of Commons*

E MONAR PIE

1 shortcrust flan case, cooked
1 large onion, chopped very fine
2 oz. butter or dripping
1 heaped tablespoon flour
chopped chicken, turkey, ham or lamb
slices of tomato
selection of cooked left-over vegetables (potatoes, peas, carrots, cauliflower), diced
chicken stock
salt, pepper
French mustard
grated cheese
breadcrumbs

Sauter onion in the butter or dripping till soft but not brown, remove from heat and add flour. Gradually add stock until it becomes a thickish sauce. Add half the grated cheese to sauce, with the French mustard and seasoning. Add all the diced meat and vegetables.

Adjust consistency and pour into flan case, cover with slices of tomato and sprinkle with the rest of cheese and breadcrumbs. Put in oven until hot and crispy on top.

30 mins — Own invention

Serves 6-8 — *Mrs Colin Stroyan, Killin*

E F CHICKEN CURRY

1 chicken
2 oz. ghee, butter or cooking oil
1 pint stock or water
½ teaspoon salt
4 teaspoons ground onions
1 teaspoon ground turmeric
½ teaspoon ground chili
½ teaspoon ground ginger
¼ teaspoon ground garlic
½ teaspoon ground coriander

Take a medium sized chicken and divide into 16 pieces. Melt ghee, butter or oil, and as soon as it begins to bubble throw in ground onion and cook until golden. Add remainder of ground ingredients and stir until brown. Put in pieces of chicken and salt and cook to a light brown colour. Add stock or water, cover with tight fitting lid and simmer until the liquid is reduced by half. This should take from half to three quarters of an hour, by which time the dish is ready to be served.

Personally I use chicken of about 3 lbs. or just over. I use butter and chicken stock, and I do not put in a full half teaspoon chili as I find that for my taste this tends to dominate the flavour and kill the gentle aroma of the other spices. The recipe is very good as given and eaten hot, but if you want real food fit for the gods take the flesh off the bones while still hot, put in flat dish, cover with the juice and leave in fridge overnight. Eat cold next day with a salad.

30 mins
Serves 6 *W. H. Rankin, Glenalmond*

E F CHICKEN, DEEP FRIED

1 chicken joint per person	grated rind of 1 lemon
3 tablespoons flour	salt, pepper
3 tablespoons parsley	mixture of oil and butter for baking
2 teaspoons tarragon	tin of soup (optional)
2 teaspoons rosemary	

Heat oven to 400° and melt fat in roasting tin.

In a bowl combine the flour, parsley, tarragon, rosemary, lemon rind, salt and pepper. Coat chicken joints in as much of this mixture as it will hold, lay joints side by side in the hot fat. Pour any remaining coating mixture over the top.

Roast for about ¾ hour, or until tender and very crisp. Baste at intervals, but do not turn the joints. If a gravy is needed, pour off all but a very little of the surplus fat from tin when the chicken has been removed, and add a tin of soup, preferably condensed. Chicken soup is very good, and mushroom or celery are equally good if preferred.

15 mins *Mrs John Horsfall, Kinloch Rannoch*

BAKED CHICKEN WITH PEACHES

4 oz. butter	3 teacups cornflakes, crushed
½ teaspoon salt	1 16 oz. can peach halves
freshly milled pepper	dried rosemary or thyme
4 chicken joints	

Melt butter, add salt and pepper. Dip chicken joints first into melted butter and then into crushed cornflakes, pressing coating on firmly. Place joints in shallow roasting tin, skin side up and not touching each other. Pour over remaining butter. Cook in moderate oven, 355° or gas mark 4, for 1 hour or until tender. During baking baste with hot butter, but do not turn joints. About 15 mins before end of cooking add drained peach halves, spoon over a little peach juice, and return to oven to finish cooking. Before serving sprinkle peaches with crushed dried rosemary or thyme.

Serves 4 *Mrs A. M. Robertson, Dunkeld*

NF CHICKEN WITH CHANTERELLES

From late July towards the end of the year you can wander through the woods and come home with a basket of chanterelles. With half a pound of these and the following ingredients you can make a simple but delicious dish.

1 free range chicken	½ pint cream
4 oz. butter	glass of malt whisky (optional)

Melt the butter in a thick casserole and brown the chicken, sprinkling it with about half the malt whisky (I would not use a blend). Remove the chicken from the pan, and sauter the chanterelles which you have cleaned, dried and sliced or chopped. Pour in the rest of the whisky, stir to amalgamate the juices. Return the chicken to the casserole. Pour in the cream, which should be heated, and simmer until the chicken is cooked. Baste occasionally. The time required will depend on the size of the chicken. Check the seasoning, and serve chicken and sauce separately. Little new potatoes go well with this, and if you want a vegetable it should be kept very simple. You will find that the chicken and sauce taste wonderfully of the woods where you gathered the chanterelles, and it is a pity to spoil the subtle flavour.

A fruity German or Alsation wine goes well with this dish. Because of the cream in this dish it is advisable to follow it with a sharp but light pudding. A traditional raspberry tart is very good.

15-20 mins
Serves 4-6

Probably a traditional French recipe
Colin H. Hamilton, Foss

E TANDOORI CHICKEN

2 chickens about $1\frac{1}{2}$ lb. each
1 tablespoon clarified butter
1 large raw onion
2 lemons or limes

marinade made of:
1 teaspoon ground saffron
1 teaspoon red chillie powder
juice of 2 lemons or limes
1 teaspoon salt
2 cloves garlic, crushed
2 teaspoons coriander
1 teaspoon ground cumin seeds
1 carton yoghurt

Wash and skin chickens. Make cuts on the breast and legs. Mix together all the marinade ingredients and rub well into chickens, inserting into the cuts. Leave for 12 hours.

Place chickens on trivet in a baking tray and roast in a very hot oven until tender. Baste occasionally with melted clarified butter. Serve hot with raw sliced onions and quartered lemons or limes.

If serving rice with this dish, add to the rice: cloves, a stick of cinnamon, black pepper and cardamon seeds. Remove, when rice is cooked and before serving, the cloves and stick of cinnamon.

10 mins
Serves 6-8

Mrs Maitland-Smith, Dunkeld

CHICKEN WITH CREAM AND ASPARAGUS SAUCE

6 chicken joints
3 oz. butter
1 glass white wine
$\frac{1}{3}$ pint or 1 teacup chicken stock – use water and $\frac{1}{2}$ chicken stock cube
salt, pepper
1 level tablespoon flour
$\frac{1}{4}$ pint cream
4 oz. button mushrooms, trimmed and sliced
1 tin asparagus tips
Parmesan cheese

Heat 2 oz. of the butter in a large deep saucepan. When melted add the chicken joints and slowly brown all over without burning the butter, turning the chicken frequently. Add the wine, stock and seasoning, cover with a lid and simmer gently for about 20 mins.

Meanwhile sauter the button mushrooms quickly in $\frac{1}{2}$ oz. of the remaining butter and drain on to a plate ready for use. Mix together remaining butter with the flour on a plate and set aside. Arrange cooked chicken joints flesh side upwards on a large oval ovenproof serving platter and place in the oven to keep warm. Reduce the sauce in the pan a little and then add the cream and mixed butter and flour. Stir well until thickened and boiling.

Add pre-heated asparagus tips and sauté mushrooms to the sauce, spoon over the chicken in the dish. Sprinkle with parmesan cheese and pass under a hot grill until browned. Serve at once.

The chicken can be cooked before the guests arrive and kept hot in the oven during cocktail time; the sauce can be added just before serving.

Serves 6 *Mrs Kenneth Ireland, Pitlochry*

F CHICKEN NOODLE CASSEROLE

8 oz. egg noodles
12 oz. cooked chicken (cubed)
1½ oz. margarine
1 tin tomato soup
2 sticks celery, chopped
¼ pint rosé wine
½ green pepper
1 onion, chopped
3 sprigs of parsley
1 slice bread (torn in pieces)
1 oz. Cheddar cheese

Cook noodles, put in casserole. Scatter chicken over noodles, and dot with butter. Blend soup, celery, wine, green pepper, onion, salt and parsley for 10 seconds in blender, pour over chicken and noodles.
Drop bread and cheese through hole in lid of blender goblet, sprinkle over dish. Bake at 350° until lightly browned and bubbly.

Serves 4-5 *Miss Katrina Gruer, Edinburgh*

E F CHICKEN DIVAN

2 pkts. frozen broccoli
2 tins cream of chicken soup
2 cups sliced cooked chicken
1 tablespoon melted butter
½ teaspoon curry powder
1 teaspoon lemon juice
½ cup strong Cheddar cheese
½ cup soft breadcrumbs
1 cup mayonnaise

Cook broccoli, arrange in a buttered ovenproof casserole, place sliced chicken on top of broccoli. Combine soup, lemon juice, mayonnaise, curry powder and pour over the chicken. Sprinkle with cheese and top with breadcrumbs.
Cook in oven at 350° for 25-30 mins.
Savoury rice or baked potatoes are good with this dish.

30 mins
Serves 5-6 *Mrs G. Brown, Green Park Hotel, Pitlochry*

E NF CHICKEN WITH ALMOND SAUCE

Take 4 suprêmes of chicken. Brush with egg and roll in ground almonds, pressing in well. Cook in hot butter in a moderately hot oven (425°, gas mark 6) for 30 mins, until tender. Baste once or twice during the cooking.

Serve with almond sauce. To make this, shred 2 oz. blanched almonds, brown in ½ oz. butter, season and add ¼ pint double cream. Heat, but do not boil.

Now that frozen suprêmes of chicken are available they are, when thawed, ideal for this recipe, being tender and boneless.

10 mins
Serves 4 *Mrs J. Shaw Grant, Inverness*

ROAST DUCKLING WITH MINT AND LEMON

4-5 lb. duckling
1 tablespoon chopped mint
1 teaspoon sugar
2 oz. butter
grated rind and juice of ½ lemon
salt, pepper
¼ pint stock
1½ lemons, sliced
1 bunch watercress

Mix half the chopped mint with the sugar, 1 oz. butter, the grated rind of ½ lemon and seasoning. Place this mixture inside the duck and truss it. Place duck in a roasting tin, pour round half the stock and roast in a moderately hot oven, 400°, gas mark 6, for 15 minutes per lb. and 15 minutes over.

When the duck is cooked remove from tin and keep hot. Tip out excess fat from the roasting tin, leaving any sediment behind. Pour in the remaining stock and the juice of half a lemon, boil up and season carefully to taste. Strain this sauce through a fine strainer or piece of muslin. Add the remaining chopped mint, pour sauce over the duck.

Garnish the dish with slices of lemon and small bouquets of watercress.

30 mins
Serves 3 *Miss Joan Knight, Perth*

PHEASANT CREAM

F

1 pheasant
slices of bacon
butter for cooking
$1\frac{1}{2}$ glasses port
$\frac{1}{2}$ pint cream
Worcester sauce
salt, pepper
1 level dessertspoon flour

Put butter inside pheasant. Dust with salt and pepper. Cover with butter and bacon and roast in hot oven till 5 minutes short of being tender. Remove bacon and pour off some of the fat. Carve bird in pan and remove pieces to dish for serving. Boil up the juices in pan on top of cooker, add flour, stir in port and a good dash of Worcester sauce. Pour on cream and cook till it bubbles. Taste for seasoning and pour over pheasant.
Serve with chestnut purée.

15 mins

Serves 3-4 people *Mrs D. Hayter, Methven*

PHEASANT WITH GREEN APPLES

F

1 pheasant
$\frac{1}{4}$ lb. chopped bacon
$\frac{1}{2}$ Spanish onion, finely chopped
1 clove garlic
2 tablespoons butter
4 small cooking apples
$\frac{1}{2}$ pint cream
salt
freshly ground black pepper
4 tablespoons cointreau
2 tablespoons oil

Sauter bacon, onion and garlic in butter and oil until golden. Remove from casserole and brown pheasant. Peel, core and slice apples thickly, return all to casserole, placing apples round pheasant. Pour over 4 tablespoons cointreau. Simmer for 10 mins, covered. Stir in cream and seasoning and cook in a slow oven at 275° until pheasant is tender.
Before serving place pheasant and bacon bits in a clean casserole. Purée the remaining ingredients and pour over pheasant.
This is a good way of using up old birds or deep frozen ones. If deep frozen they should not be re-frozen.

Serves 4-6 *Mrs John H. Christie, Glenfarg*

E PHEASANT WITH CHESTNUTS

1 pheasant (plucked and drawn)
1 tablespoon olive oil
1 oz. butter
½ lb. chestnuts, peeled
2 medium onions, sliced
3 level tablespoons flour
¾ pint stock
1 wine glass Burgundy
salt, pepper
grated rind and juice of ½ orange
2 teaspoons red currant jelly
bouquet garni
chopped parsley

Fry pheasant in fat for 6 minutes until golden brown. Remove with a slatted spoon, place in an ovenproof casserole. Fry chestnuts and onions in the fat for 5 minutes until golden brown, add to meat. Stir flour into remaining fat and cook for 3 minutes. Remove pan from heat, add stock and wine gradually. Bring to the boil, stir until thickened. Season and pour over pheasant. Add orange rind and juice, red currant jelly and bouquet garni. Cover, cook in the centre of oven at 350°, gas mark 4, for 1 hour until pheasant is tender. Remove bouquet garni and re-season if necessary. Serve sprinkled with chopped parsley.

Mrs Mary C. Annandale, Perth

F CASSEROLE OF PHEASANT

1 pheasant
1 large onion, sliced
water
salt
½ pint cream
rolls fried bacon
fried mushrooms

Pluck and draw pheasant. Partially roast bird for about 30 mins so that meat can be removed easily from the bone. Lay this aside in flat casserole.

Take carcase and place in stewpan with large sliced onion, cover with water, stew until stock is reduced to ½ pint. Strain off stock, season lightly with salt, add ½ pint cream and thicken with arrowroot or cornflour. Pour this sauce over the meat in

the casserole and cook slowly for about ¾ hour (or until cooked). If sauce dries add more cream or stock.
Serve in casserole, garnish with rolls of fried bacon and mushrooms fried in butter.

Serves 6 *Miss Diana Dixon, J.P., Louth, Lincolnshire*

E NF

SAXON PUDDING

The hot weather over the last few years has meant that there are now many more partridges on sale, but contrarily should you fail to find any then try the pudding substituting old grouse.
Line a well-greased 2-pint basin with suet crust. Joint a partridge and roll in seasoned flour with ¼ lb. rump steak cut in 1″ cubes, place in the basin with 2 oz. coarsely chopped mushrooms, and 1 tablespoon of finely chopped parsley and a pinch of dried mixed herbs. Pour over 5 fl. oz. Burgundy and top up with chicken stock. Cover with a pastry lid and buttered greaseproof and then tie round a cloth. Place in a pan of boiling water and steam for 3 hours.

30 mins
Serves 4

Mrs R. S. Stewart-Wilson, Tullymet

PTARMIGAN

The finest dish that any Icelander like myself can be offered is pot-roasted ptarmigan with sugared potatoes – especially as prepared by my mother.
The trouble is that she is one of these culinary geniuses who cooks by instinct rather than by formula or recipe. It took a lot of work to wring this recipe out of her!

- 2-3 ptarmigan, skinned not plucked
- 2-3 rashers fat bacon
- 60 grams butter
- 2 decilitres boiling water
- 2 decilitres boiled milk

For the sauce:

liquor from the boiling
30 gr. butter
30 gr. flour
2-3 dl. whipped cream
sauce colouring
salt
red currant jelly

The ptarmigan, which should have been hung for at least a week, should be thoroughly cleaned and dried after skinning. Preserve the heart and gizzard, suitably prepared; discard liver and crop. Tie a rasher of fat bacon over each breast. Melt the butter in the cooking pot and fry the ptarmigan lightly until brown, with hearts and gizzards. Add the boiling water and boiling milk, and simmer gently for 1-1½ hours. Half way through remove the bacon. If required turn the birds to ensure even cooking.
For the sauce melt the butter in a separate pot. Add the liquor from the ptarmigan after mixing flour into the butter. Add colouring, salt, and a dash of red currant jelly to taste. The sauce should be fairly thick. Just before serving add the whipped cream. The birds, which should have been kept warm in their pot, should be briefly heated in the sauce before serving.
The birds can be served either whole or halved. Wings and legs can also be served separately.

sugared potatoes:

½ kg. small potatoes
60 gr. sugar
40 gr. butter

The potatoes should be boiled, peeled and placed in a sieve. Brown the sugar gently in a frying pan, taking care not to let it get too dark. Add butter and stir vigorously. Run cold water over the potatoes and put them in the frying pan. Shake and stir the pan well as the potatoes are coated and heated.
Serve, ideally, with red cabbage.
All this takes great dexterity and at least three hands. But when done, just sit back and enjoy the beatific look on the faces of your guests. It's really worth it.

Serves 3-4 *Magnus Magnusson, Glasgow*

F SWEET SOUR RABBIT

- 2 lbs. jointed prepared rabbit (or fowl)
- 6 oz. onions, sliced
- ½ pint chicken stock (or cube)
- ½ pint dry white wine (or beer)
- 1 bay leaf
- 2 teaspoons red currant jelly
- 8 prunes
- 2 oz. raisins
- 1 tablespoon malt vinegar
- 1 teaspoon cornflour
- salt
- pepper
- garnish

Marinade rabbit with onions in the wine for 6-12 hours, stirring occasionally. Remove onions. Add prunes, red currant jelly, chicken stock and seasoning, and cook until tender. This will take about 1½ hours at 320°, or gas mark 3.

Blend cornflour in vinegar, add to stew, boil to thicken. Should be served with all bones removed, covered with thickened sauce, and topped with chopped nuts and freshly chopped parsley. The prune stones and bay leaf should also be removed before the dish is brought to the table.

Serves 4-6 *Mrs Campbell Adamson, Brechin*

CASSEROLE OF VENISON, GHILLIES' STYLE

- 1 lb. shoulder venison
- 4 large carrots, diced
- 4 large onions, diced
- 1 small kale, sliced
- 2 oz. flour
- ¼ pint oil
- seasoning
- small jar red currant jelly
- ¼ lb. mushrooms, sliced
- small head celery, sliced
- 2 cups red wine
- 1 small glass port
- 1½ pints beef stock

Cut venison into cubes and marinade overnight in wine, oil, salt and pepper, and some sliced onion. A little garlic may be added.

Sauter venison and vegetables together until brown in 2 tablespoons oil. Add flour, cook out flour. Then add $1\frac{1}{2}$ pints beef stock and the marinade. Braise in a moderate oven till tender. Finish by adding port and red currant jelly. Garnish with sprigs of parsley and croutons.

Serves 4-6 *Lawrence Healy, Chef, Pitlochry Hydro Hotel*

NF **ROAST HAUNCH OF VENISON**

Marinade meat for at least 2 hours in a French dressing of 4 parts oil to 1 part vinegar, chopped herbs, salt and pepper.
Prepare pastry. Sift 5 lb. flour with 2 oz. salt. Rub in 10 oz. margarine or lard, mix in 2 pints water to make a smooth dough. Roll out dough to an oblong shape to take the haunch, making it about $\frac{1}{4}$″ thick. Remove haunch from marinade and wrap it completely in the paste, sealing all joins up carefully.
Cook in the oven at 400° for first 20 minutes, then lower heat to 350° and roast for $2\frac{1}{4}$-$2\frac{3}{4}$ hours, depending on size.
Break open the crust, drain off gravy which will have collected inside, lift out haunch on to serving dish.
This is the best way I know of roasting venison, which is apt to be dry if cooked in the normal way. The pastry amount given would cover a very large haunch of 10-12 lb.

Serves at least 8 *Mrs H. M. McBride, Aberfeldy*

BRAINS

This is a recipe for my favourite food, unfortunately not available in most restaurants. In France, it is called Cervelles, in Italy it is Cervella. In Scotland it is just Brains. It is an old Scottish dish, but I find nowadays that I get it more readily on the continent or in Soho, where I eat it under the plaque which says that here John Logie Baird invented television. He had brains too.

I've never cooked anything but a coddled egg myself, but this recipe makes a new man of me.

Start with sheep's brains (or calve's brains will do, but they are not so delicate). Put them for 12 hours under running water to purify them.

Boil them in a small pot of water, with salt and pepper, bay leaf, carrots, onions and the juice of half a lemon. Blanch the brains and, when they are cool, take off the skin.

Fry the brains in deep oil, but it must be really good oil. Switch 2 eggs, salt and pepper and chopped parsley. Put this mixture through dry flour and fry. Keep frying because it must be served very hot. Serve the brains sprinkled with lemon juice.

This to my mind is the most delicate dish in the world. I like to drink, with the brains, a Sicilian wine, Corvo Salaparuta. The Mafia are paying all my expenses.

Jack House, Glasgow

E F

SWEETBREADS

Soak 4 lb. ox sweetbreads in salted water overnight. Blanch thoroughly and remove all skin, etc. Place in a casserole, add a pinch salt and pepper, and cover with mixture of Burgundy or a good consommé. Add slivers of zest of orange. Cook covered in oven until a fork will slip through the sweetbreads.

When required – and all the preceding can be done well in advance – put some Burgundy in a suitable saucepan with tomato purée. Stir well, add sliced mushrooms and sweetbreads, and heat slowly until sweetbreads are once again easily pierced with a fork.

Own invention

Serves 8-10 *Robin Duff, Meldrum, Aberdeenshire*

E NF KIDNEYS L'ORANGE

4 lambs' kidneys
1 orange
1 tablespoon tomato ketchup
1 port glass brandy
1 onion
salt, pepper
12 oz. long grain rice
1 tablespoon oil
6 tablespoons single cream
¼ pint cream

Skin, halve, remove core and soak kidneys for ½ hour in salted water. Drain and cut into ½ inch strips. Marinade kidneys in all remaining ingredients except onions and cream. Place in fridge for 2 hours.
Drain kidneys and reserve juice. Fry in oil for 5 mins. Remove and keep hot in serving dish.
Finely chop onions and fry in same oil. Add marinade and mix well. Simmer for 5 mins. Add cream, removing from heat, otherwise it will curdle, and pour over kidneys.
Serve with fluffy buttered rice and green side salad.

20 mins
Serves 4 *Mrs Turk, Fasganeon Hotel, Pitlochry*

E CONTINENTAL LIVER

½ lb. liver
½ lb. bacon
2 tablespoons breadcrumbs
1 tablespoon chopped parsley
1 tablespoon chopped onion
¼ tablespoon grated lemon rind
1 cup stock or water
1 tablespoon Worcester sauce
½ teaspoon salt

Wash liver, cut in slices ½ inch thick. Place on well greased baking tin. Mix all dry ingredients and sprinkle over liver. Cover with slices of bacon. Pour stock over, bake in moderate oven for 45 mins. Finally add Worcester sauce to gravy.

15 mins English/Tamil, South India, cookery book
Serves 4 *Mrs E. W. Anstey, Dunkeld*

E CASSEROLE OF KIDNEY AND SAUSAGE

$1\frac{1}{2}$ lb. kidney (any kind)	2 carrots
$\frac{1}{2}$ lb. pork sausages	1 onion
1 level tablespoon flour	4 oz. mushrooms
salt, pepper	1 stock cube
2 oz. fat or oil	$\frac{1}{2}$ pint hot water

Cut kidney into small pieces, removing core and any skin. Cut each sausage into 3 pieces. Mix seasoning and flour and roll kidney and sausage in this to coat them.

Scrape and cut carrots, peel and slice onions, slice mushrooms. Crumble stock cube in hot water. Melt fat or oil in pan or casserole and fry meat for a few minutes. Remove and fry carrots and onions, add stock cube fluid and stir until it boils. Add meat and mushrooms. Cover and simmer until kidney is tender, approx. 2 hours.

Take care not to fry kidney for too long as it can become tough and hard. It just needs to be browned lightly. This dish will reheat well, but bring it to the boil.

30 mins
Serves 4-6

Mrs R. Dalziel, Murthly

E SWEET-SOUR TONGUE

Boil 1 large ox tongue, or 6 small calves' or lambs' tongues, in salted water until tender. A few vegetables such as carrot, onion, celery, and a bay leaf, help to give the stock a good flavour. Boiling time will be up to 2 hours for the larger tongue. Keep the stock as this makes a good soup base. When cool enough to handle, skin, and trim away the gristly part.

Melt 1 oz. butter in a large pan, and in it brown 1 chopped onion, 1 chopped carrot, a diced rasher of bacon, garlic and about 2 teaspoons parsley. After the tongue has been skinned, cut it into slices $\frac{1}{2}$ inch thick and add these to the pan to brown.

When they are well coloured, sprinkle in 1 dessertspoon of flour, 2 tablespoons vinegar (not malt vinegar as it is too rough), the same amount of stock that the tongue was cooked in, and salt and pepper. Mix well together, turn the slices, add 1 tablespoon sugar, a bay leaf and 1 teaspoon raisins.
Cook gently, uncovered, until the sauce has reduced and thickened a little. Taste at this stage, add more sugar or vinegar, according to whether you prefer the sauce to be more sweet or more sharp. Dish up the tongue slices and pour the sauce over.

1 hour
Serves 6 *Mrs R. Robertson, Pitlochry*

SALADS, SAUCES, SAVOURIES, EGG DISHES

SUMMER SALAD

4 large tomatoes
1 large cucumber
1 large green pepper
4 oz. black olives
4 oz. white cheese
parsley
$\frac{1}{4}$ pint oil and vinegar
seasoning

Peel the tomatoes and quarter, and cut the unpeeled cucumber down the middle and quarter it. Remove any large pips and cut into 1-inch lengths. Halve pepper and remove pips, cut into narrow strips. Halve and stone olives, chop cheese into cubes. Mix together in a bowl and coat with oil and vinegar mixed together.

Season, sprinkle with parsley and refrigerate for at least 3 hours.

Mrs Gerald Colin, Louth, Lincolnshire

E APPLE AND CELERY MAYONNAISE

approx. 1 eating apple per person
equal quantity of celery
mayonnaise

Peel and core apples. If red skinned, leave one or two unpeeled. Cut into smallish dice, dice an equal quantity of crisp sticks of celery.

Mix apples and celery together and coat well with mayonnaise. Serve in individual dishes with brown bread and butter, or as part of an hors d'oeuvres.

Mrs H. Ford, Stanley

E NF APPLE AND ONION MAYONNAISE

apple
onion
2 eggs
½ teaspoon mustard
1 dessertspoon sugar
½ teaspoon salt and pepper
1 tablespoon vinegar

Put all ingredients into a mixer and mix well. When well mixed add olive oil drop by drop until thick, add a little cream. Chop onion and apple finely, add to mayonnaise sauce. ¾ teaspoon curry powder may be added if wished.

10 mins

Mrs Stewart-Stevens, Moulin

E NF POTATO SALAD

12 potatoes, boiled in skins, peeled and cubed ½″ x ½″ x ½″
1 cup chopped celery
1 cup chopped onion, inc. some spring onions
2 cucumbers, chopped and added when ready to be served
1 single recipe of salad dressing below
hard-boiled eggs
tomato wedges

Make salad dressing, add and stir warm into diced potatoes, celery and onions. Refrigerate for as long as 3 days. Before serving add cucumbers, hard-boiled egg slices and tomato wedges.

Cooked salad dressing:

1½ teaspoons dry mustard
4 tablespoons gran. sugar
½ teaspoon salt
2 eggs
¼ pint cider vinegar
2 tablespoons butter
12 oz. can evaporated milk

Cook all together, omitting milk and butter, until the mixture thickens. Then add the butter. When cool add can of evaporated milk.

Mrs Herbert Neal
At least 100 years ago

1 hour
Serves 20

Mrs R. T. A. Ross, Pitlochry

E NF AVOCADO SALAD

- $\frac{3}{4}$ - 1 lb. shredded white cabage or Chinese leaves
- 1-2 tablespoons onion, grated
- 4 small carrots, sliced small
- 2 oz. shelled walnuts, roughly broken
- 4 tomatoes, roughly chopped
- 4 hard-boiled eggs, sliced
- 1 large ripe avocado pear
- French dressing

Put everything except the avocado into a large bowl and mix well. Peel and dice avocado just before meal or it will go brown. Toss in the dressing and add to the salad, making sure the whole thing is well seasoned – with black pepper and sea salt if possible. *Serves four enormous portions. Very popular and satisfying main dish with brown bread and butter.*

20 mins
Serves 4

Gabriel Woolf, London

MUSHROOMS IN MUSTARD

- 1 lb. button mushrooms
- juice of 1 lemon
- 8 tablespoons olive oil
- 6 black peppercorns
- 2 bay leaves
- 1 tablespoon Dijon mustard
- salt
- chopped parsley

Wash and drain mushrooms. Cut into halves or quarters. Marinade in lemon juice, olive oil, peppercorns and bay leaves for at least 8 hours (I leave them for $1\frac{1}{2}$ days).
To make mustard sauce, mix 4-6 tablespoons marinade juices with Dijon mustard and shake until well blended in a small jar. Add salt, and a little more lemon juice or olive oil if required. *I always find there is never enough juice to mix with mustard, and I always add more olive oil and lemon juice. Whilst mushrooms are marinading, cover dish and give it a good shake-up each time you pass. This makes more juice.*

Always a favourite and easy to prepare. Very good as barbecue salad, for cold buffet, or as a starter on its own, served with French bread.

Mrs A. G. Godson, Headley, Hants

CRAB SALAD

1 medium crab per person
1 hard-boiled egg per person
wine vinegar
olive oil
radishes
dry mustard
salt
ground black pepper
chopped parsley

Flake crab meat into a bowl, add chopped egg whites. Mash yolks with wine vinegar, olive oil, dry mustard and pepper. Stir into crab, taste and add salt. Add parsley. Scrub and dry crab body shells, fill with mixture and decorate with sliced radishes. Serve on lettuce leaves with dry biscuits.

30 mins

Mrs R. Rorie, Laide

E NF CUCUMBER AND SOUR CREAM SAUCE

1 carton sour cream
½ cucumber
1 hard-boiled egg
½ tablespoon finely chopped parsley
1 teaspoon lemon juice
salt, pepper, pinch of cayenne
½ teaspoon chopped fresh dill if available

Peel cucumber and coarsely grate flesh. Place cucumber in a sieve, sprinkle lightly with salt and leave it to sweat for half an hour. Drain off excess liquid and pat the cucumber dry with a clean cloth.

Blend lemon juice into sour cream. Finely chop the hard-boiled egg and add it to the sauce with the parsley and cucumber. Season with salt and pepper.

Spoon the sauce into a serving dish and top with a light dusting of cayenne, and the dill if you have it, but this is entirely optional. *This is excellent with cold salmon.*

20 mins
Serves 4-6 *Mrs Charles Findlay, Killiecrankie*

E COLD CURRY MAYONNAISE

1 onion
1 tablespoon curry powder
lemon juice
1 dessertspoon brown sugar
½ pint double cream
1 glass red wine
½ pint mayonnaise

Fry an onion till golden brown in olive oil, add curry powder, lemon juice, brown sugar and glass of red wine. Liquidise or sieve, add the mayonnaise and cream.
Season to taste. *Cover chicken or turkey, and it is very good for prawn cocktail.*

20 mins
Serves 4-6 *Mrs J. K. Rodwell, Scone*

E SALAD DRESSING

1 teaspoon salt
2 teaspoons mustard
1 tablespoon sugar
1 tablespoon flour
2 egg yolks
1½ tablespoons melted butter
¼ cup vinegar (preferably cider vinegar)
¾ cup milk
cayenne pepper

Mix dry ingredients, add egg yolks, milk and vinegar very slowly. Cook over boiling water until mixture thickens.
This dressing will keep for some weeks in bottles. Mix as required with a little sour cream, plain yoghurt or the top of the milk.

Indian/English cook book
15 mins *Mrs E. W. Anstey, Dunkeld*

F ALL PURPOSE TOMATO SAUCE

1 large onion, finely chopped
4 carrots, finely chopped
1 clove garlic, finely chopped
1 tablespoon olive oil
1 heaped tablespoon butter
1 heaped tablespoon plain flour
stock, left-over wine
shake of Worcester sauce
2 lb. fresh tomatoes or large tin peeled tomatoes
1 dessertspoon sugar
pinch thyme and rosemary
½ teaspoon ground ginger
salt, black pepper
bouillon cube
minced parsley
cream

Using a heavy pan fry onions, garlic and sliced carrots in a mixture of olive oil and butter till golden. Take off heat to cool and add flour until all the butter has been absorbed. Stir well till light brown, add stock, left-over wine or milk gradually, till the sauce boils and the consistency is correct. Peel and pip tomatoes and add these, with sugar, thyme, rosemary, Worcester sauce, salt, stock cube, black pepper and ginger. Stir well and adjust seasoning. Add fresh cream and minced parsley.
Very good over spaghetti, on top of moussaka or over grilled fillets of trout, plaice and sole. It is a wonderful standby, and if thinned down with cream and sherry makes an excellent home-made tomato soup.

Mrs Colin Stroyan, Killin

E F SAUCE DOBSON

2 oz. butter
2 shallots, browned
½ pint hot water with 1 meat cube
curry powder
2 tomatoes or 1 small tin tomato purée
2 tablespoons coconut
1 apple
cream

Cook all ingredients together gently for ¾ hour. Liquidise. Add 1 heaped tablespoon curry powder and some cream to taste. Serve with boiled chicken, fish or boiled ham.

Mrs Barbara Leburn, Gateside

QUICK HOLLANDAISE SAUCE

Put 4 egg yolks, 2 tablespoons lemon juice and a pinch of cayenne pepper in to blender and whisk at slow speed. Remove cap and pour in one cup boiling butter in a steady stream till the yolks have thickened. Switch off and serve at once.

This is delicious and so easy. It can be done at the last minute, just as the candles are being lit on the table. But be careful not to make the butter too hot or it will curdle the egg yolks. On the other hand if the butter is not hot enough the sauce will not thicken.

Mrs Colin Stroyan, Killin

E NF STUFFING FOR PHEASANT

Remove carcase bones, leaving legs and wings. Make stuffing as follows:

- 2 oz. butter
- small onion
- ½ lb. streaky bacon, finely chopped
- 1 dessert apple
- 1 teacup fresh breadcrumbs
- ½ lb. fresh spinach or cabbage
- 1 teaspoon sage and thyme, chopped
- salt, pepper

Cook onion in butter but do not colour. Add rest of ingredients. Stuff pheasant back into shape and secure with skewers or by stitching.

Put sliced dessert apple on top of bird with some butter, bake for 45-60 mins at 400°. Add cream and sherry to gravy.

Serves 2 *Mrs T. C. Donald, Pitlochry*

ASPIC JELLY

- quart well-flavoured beef stock
- 1 oz. gelatine
- herbs
- ¼ cup sherry
- 1 teaspoon vinegar
- 1 egg, complete with shell

Whisk the mixture until it comes to the boil, stand for 15 mins. Strain through flannel and allow to set.

Aspic jelly can of course also be bought ready made.

Miss M. Douglas, Ballinluig

ORANGE PRESERVE

8 oranges
4 cups sugar
1 cup vinegar
½ cup water
10 cloves
2 sticks cinnamon

Slice oranges, cover with water and simmer for 1 hour. Drain, keeping liquid. Boil liquid with sugar, vinegar and spices for 5 minutes, then add oranges and simmer for 1 hour until fruit looks glazed. Pack into jars and top up with syrup. Seal jars when cool and keep as jam or chutney.

Very good to serve with all game, whether roasted or casseroled.

Mrs J. P. Rettie, Crianlarich

E NF WHITE SAUCE, SWEET

1 oz. butter
1 oz. flour
½-1 pint milk
1 oz. castor sugar
few drops vanilla essence

Melt butter in pan, stir in flour. Add milk and sugar, stir until smooth and boil for several minutes, stirring all the time. Lastly add flavouring.

This white sauce is ideal for serving with Christmas and other puddings. The unusual flavour is achieved by the use of ordinary flour and not cornflour.

Grandmother's recipe
Leon Sinden, Perth

NF CARAMEL CREAM SAUCE

3 oz. sugar
lemon juice
2 small cups cream

Boil sugar to a caramel with water in the usual way, add a few drops of lemon juice, and immediately pour over 1 small cup of cream. Leave till cold. Whip another cup of cream and add to the caramel when cold. Pour over the pudding.

Delicious over any cold cream pudding or soufflé.

The Hon. Mrs John Boyle, Dunkeld

E F HOT CHOCOLATE SAUCE

$\frac{1}{4}$ lb. butter
$\frac{1}{2}$ cup cocoa powder
1 cup soft brown sugar
4 tablespoons water

Melt the ingredients in a double boiler, stirring occasionally. Allow to simmer until well mixed. Serve with ice cream.
This mixture can be adapted easily by adding nuts, raisins, rum or brandy and, by omitting the cocoa powder, becomes butter-scotch sauce. Reheats well in a double boiler.

10 mins
Serves 6-8 *Sir Douglas Haddow, Edinburgh*

E NF CHEESE AND HAM PIE

10 oz. shortcrust pastry
8 oz. cooked ham, diced
8 oz. Cheddar cheese, diced
1 large onion, finely chopped
2 eggs, beaten
salt, pepper
a little milk for glazing

Roll out two thirds of pastry and line a greased 1 lb. loaf tin. Mix ham, cheese, onion and egg together and season. Pour into lined tin, pressing down well.
Roll out remaining pastry to $\frac{1}{4}$ inch thick, damp edges and cover top of pie, using trimmings to decorate. Glaze top with milk and bake in a fairly hot oven (400°, gas mark 6) for 1 hour. Allow to cool in tin before removing.

20 mins
Serves 6-8 *Mrs M. Riddell, Glenlyon*

E NF STUFFED HAM ROLLS

Allow 2 slices of ham and 1 egg per person. Boil eggs for 10 mins. Cool and put through a mincer. Add mayonnaise, curry powder, cayenne pepper, garlic powder, ready-made mustard, salt, pepper, savoury seasoning, chopped parsley and chopped chives. Mix well.

It is impossible to say how much of the above to use, as it all depends on how many eggs are being used. The idea is to add and taste until it is as you like it. You never make the same flavour twice. The mixture should be kept fairly stiff so that it stays in the roll of ham, and if it is made the day before it is needed the flavour will be improved.

30 mins

Lady Fraser, Dunblane

NF MUSHROOM SAVOURIES

- $\frac{1}{2}$ lb. mushrooms
- 1 oz. butter
- 1 dessertspoon oil
- 2 tablespoons spring onions
- 1 teaspoon flour
- $\frac{1}{4}$ pint cream
- 1 tablespoon sherry
- salt, pepper

Sauter mushrooms in hot butter and oil for 4 mins, but do not brown. Add spring onions and toss over moderate heat for 2 mins. Stir in the flour and cook slowly for 2 mins.
Away from the heat blend in the cream and seasonings. Then boil down rapidly till the cream has reduced and thickened. Add the sherry and boil briefly. Serve on toast.

15 mins
Serves 2

Mrs Mackinlay, Dullatur

E

HOLIDAY STEW WITH CHEESE DUMPLINGS

potatoes, carrots and onions for each person
15 oz. tin tomato soup
stock or water
seasoning
15 oz. tin baked beans
cold meat scraps
all savoury left-overs as at the end of the holidays

Dumplings:
4 oz. self-raising flour
1 oz. butter or marg
2 oz. or more grated cheese
milk to mix

Prepare and slice the vegetables and cook them all together in a large saucepan in the soup and at least an equal quantity of stock or water. When they are cooked test the liquid for flavour and add seasoning as necessary. Add beans and all the left-overs and return gently to the boil.

Dumplings: Rub fat into flour and add the other ingredients, using just enough milk to make a firm dough. Form dumplings by rolling small pieces gently in floured hands, rather smaller than a ping-pong ball. Drop these on top of the simmering liquid and cover pan. Cook for about 15 mins and serve straight from the pan.
The dumplings can be omitted, in which case thicken the gravy by adding to it a crumb-like mixture made from an equal weight of flour and fat rubbed together. Stir this in carefully and it will thicken the stew. Invented on a wet half-closing day at end of caravan holiday.

Mrs R. D. Sylvester, Aberfeldy

E NF SOUFFLE AU FROMAGE

1½ oz. butter
1 oz. flour
½ pint less 4 tablespoons milk
salt, pepper, dry mustard
2 oz. Parmesan cheese, finely grated
1-2 oz. gruyère cheese, finely grated
4 eggs, separated

Butter a 1½-pint soufflé dish and place on baking tin. Heat oven to 375°, gas mark 5. Melt butter in medium-sized saucepan, stir in flour, add milk and whisk with a small wire whisk until smooth and boiling. Simmer for 3-4 minutes, then remove from heat. Beat in the cheese and egg yolks one at a time, and seasoning to taste. This basic mixture can be made in advance.
Whisk the egg whites till stiff but not dry, stir 1 large tablespoon into the mixture. Fold in the remainder lightly and quickly with a metal spoon. Immediately turn into prepared dish. Bake in centre of oven for 25-30 minutes or until lightly set and golden brown. Serve at once.

20 mins
Serves 4

Mrs David Gibson, Aberfeldy

F POPULAR SAVOURIES

12 oz. puff pastry
6 oz. curd cheese or Philadelphia cream cheese
½ lb. Cheddar cheese, grated
1 large egg
1 tablespoon onion, finely chopped
pinch garlic salt
black pepper

Blend cheeses in a bowl, add beaten egg and seasonings. Roll pastry to thickness of a penny and cut in rounds about 4″ in diameter. Put a dessertspoon of mixture in the middle, fold over and seal into a crescent. Place on baking sheet and refrigerate or freeze until required.
Brush with milk or egg and bake in hot oven for 15 mins.

Serves 8

Mrs W. G. Gordon, Blair Atholl

SPRING BAKE

- 2 cups cooked cubed ham
- 2 cups cooked rice
- ½ cup grated cheese
- ½ cup evaporated milk or light cream
- 3 tablespoons butter or marg, melted
- 1 can condensed Cream of Asparagus soup
- 2 tablespoons onion, finely chopped
- ¾ cup cornflakes, or crisps, slightly crushed

In 1½-quart casserole combine all ingredients except cornflakes and butter. Combine cornflakes and melted butter or marg and pour over mixture. Bake uncovered in moderate oven for 20-25 mins until heated through and moderately browned. Garnish with pinwheel of hot buttered asparagus.

30 mins
Serves 6

Mrs J. Watters, Pitlochry

E

POT MESS

This is something I have never forgotten from my days in H.M. Navy during the war. It is a "mopping up" or "cleaning out" dish which is used in the Navy at the end of the victualling period in order to clear out any outstanding bits and pieces, tins of, packets of, etc., etc., before the new stock comes in, and as such applies every bit as much to the housewife who finds those odds and ends in the fridge which are INDIVIDUALLY very difficult to make use of. The answer is, very simply, you get rid of them, very economically, ALL TOGETHER in one dish.

Using one of the many varieties of tinned soups as a base, and using a large iron pot – to be traditional – or saucepan, because it really doesn't matter, pop into soup base literally any food you have lying idle in the fridge – spam, bacon (fry it first), beef, potato, chicken, ANYTHING SAVOURY, cut up into small chunks. Add that last tin of peas, baked beans, tomatoes or all three – preferably all three – and cook them all together until thoroughly heated through.

Strangely and wonderfully the delicious flavour always seems to be the same, no matter how much the quantities of each "left-over" varies. It is highly nutritious, highly economical and wonderful to go to bed on. I don't mean you actually lie on it, but you know what I mean!

Rikki Fulton, Glasgow

NUT ROAST

4 oz. cashew nuts
4 oz. unsalted peanuts
4 oz. wholemeal breadcrumbs
1 medium onion
1 medium green pepper
1 tablespoon flour
little oil for frying
about ½ pint vegetable stock or water with 1½ teaspoons yeast extract dissolved in it
herbs, salt and pepper to taste

Grind nuts and breadcrumbs, chop onion and green pepper. Heat oil in a pan and gently sauter onion and pepper. Add about 1 tablespoon flour and cook for a few minutes. Gradually stir in the stock and yeast extract and cook till it thickens – but don't allow it to become too thick. Add herbs and seasoning, finally mix in the nuts and crumbs. If the mixture seems too moist add more crumbs. Put mixture into greased loaf tin and bake in oven at about 375° for 20-30 mins.
Serve with a brown gravy or tomato sauce, baked potatoes and a fresh vegetable.

Note: Nuts and breadcrumbs can be ground in some liquidisers or in a coffee grinder.

20 mins
Serves 4 *Mrs Graham Trotter, Fincastle*

E F PILCHARD SPECIAL

1 tin pilchards
4 oz. self-raising flour
½ pint milk
1 or 2 beaten eggs
1 teaspoon curry powder
1 teaspoon mixed spice
2 teaspoons soy sauce
1 oz. butter or marg
seasoning

Make a batter with flour, milk and eggs, add flavourings. Split pilchards and remove bone.

In a frying pan melt butter or marg, pour in batter, allow to cook, place pilchards on one side of the crêpe or pancake. Fold other side over. Brown under grill if pale.

Other fillings may be used, i.e. chicken, tomato and cheese, etc.

10-15 mins
Serves 4

Mrs A. Thomson, Broughty Ferry

F ICED CHEESE SOUFFLE

¾ gill cream
½ oz. Parmesan cheese
½ oz. gruyère cheese
½ gill aspic jelly
1 egg white
salt, cayenne pepper

Whip cream very slightly. Add cheeses, seasonings, liquid aspic and lastly stiffly-beaten white of egg. Pour into small papered soufflé cases or 1 larger one, freeze.

Remove band of paper, decorate with ⅓ gill cream, chervil, cress, chopped truffle, and serve.

One of the additional delights of this iced cheese soufflé is that (as one does not tell them) one's guests do not know what they are going to taste.

20 mins
Serves 2-3

The Right Hon. Anthony Stodart, North Berwick

E FAVOURITE MACARONI

½ lb. macaroni
2 oz. butter
¼ lb. ham or bacon (this must be cut into julienne strips)
¼ lb. Parmesan cheese, grated
cream
salt, pepper, nutmeg
fried breadcrumbs

Cook macaroni in butter and salted water, drain and refresh under cold tap. Melt some butter in pan and add macaroni, stir gently to remove all moisture. Add ham, or bacon well crisped. Add grated cheese, pepper, salt, grated nutmeg and 2-3 tablespoons cream.

Turn into a very hot deep dish and sprinkle the top with a good layer of breadcrumbs crisply fried, and on top of this sprinkle sieved Parmesan cheese. This must be served very hot.

Serves 4 *Mrs R. S. Stewart-Wilson, Ballinluig*

PARMESAN BACON

6 oz. green streaky bacon, cut on number 3
1 cup fine dry breadcrumbs
1 cup grated Parmesan

Remove rinds from bacon. Mix cheese and crumbs together. Dip each rasher into mixture and grill slowly until crisp.

Mrs R. S. Stewart-Wilson, Ballinluig

SWISS CHEESE FONDUE

Allow 1 wine glass white wine per person. Heat 1 teaspoon cornflour gently in wine, and add 5 oz. grated *Cheddar* cheese per person. Beat hard until it boils. Add 1 teaspoon kirsch per person, some pepper and a touch of garlic.

Serve in pan over heat at table. Cut white loaf into 1-inch squares and dip these into cheese on a fork.

I find Cheddar makes a very good fondue, and is much more digestible than proper Swiss cheese.

Mrs Barbara Liddell, Pitlochry

F QUICHE

8 oz. shortcrust pastry	fillings: smoked salmon
7 oz. Philadelphia cream cheese	shrimps
	bacon fried with onions
2 eggs, 2 extra yolks of eggs	asparagus
$\frac{1}{4}$ pint double cream	tomatoes
salt, pepper	anything you want
Parmesan cheese, grated	to use up!

Roll out pastry and line 10-inch flan case. Cream Philadelphia cheese, mix with beaten eggs, salt and pepper. Add chosen filling to pastry case, pour cheese mixture over.
Top with grated cheese and bake in a moderate oven, about 375°, for 35-40 mins.

20 mins
Serves 8 *Mrs Barbara Liddell, Pitlochry*

E NF TORTILLA

This is a recipe for a real Spanish omelette, given to me by a Spanish au pair girl.
Peel and slice very thinly 10-12 oz. raw potatoes. Finely slice a medium onion. Beat three eggs in a largish bowl, and season well. Gently sauter potatoes and onion in a large frying pan in plenty of oil. Do not brown. As each panful of potato and onion is cooked until soft, add to the bowl of eggs, with a little of the oil. Oil a small nonstick omelette pan, pour in the mixture from the bowl and cook on top of the stove until the bottom half is well set. Put in oven or under grill to cook through. The Spanish like it solid, but we preferred it just slightly runny in the centre. Loosen the bottom with a palette knife, invert serving plate over the pan and, holding both tightly together, turn pan over so that the omelette drops on to the plate.

30-40 mins Traditional Spanish recipe, given by Angelines Morgade
Serves 2-3 *Lady Balfour of Burleigh, Clackmannan*

E CHEESE PUDDING

1-2 slices bread per person (any bread, brown or white, fresh or stale)
$1\frac{1}{2}$ pints milk
4 eggs
4-6 oz. Cheddar cheese, or mixed cheeses, grated
salt, pepper
butter or marg

Thinly butter slices of bread (as for bread and butter pudding) and place in layers in ovenproof dish, putting the grated cheese between layers. Do not fill more than half way up. Beat eggs with salt and pepper and add milk. Pour over bread, leave to soak for an hour if possible, and sprinkle any remaining cheese on top.

Cook in medium oven, standing in another dish half filled with water, till set ($\frac{1}{2}$ to 1 hour). Pudding will rise slightly when cooked.

This is a filling dish and is very good served with a green salad.

First made when the sleet looked too unpleasant to venture out in, and the larder empty save for very stale bread, some stale cheese and a few eggs.

5-10 mins
Serves 4

Own invention
Mrs Kirby, Balrobin Hotel, Pitlochry

E DELICIOUS SUPPER DISH

Make a large omelette for 2 people.

Fry in oil 2 coarsely sliced onions, 2 coarsely sliced peppers, 6 skinned and chopped tomatoes, 2 cloves garlic, and some basil. Season. Add small quantity of chicken stock cube to taste and enough water to make sauce liquid. Cook till fairly tender and pour over omelette. *The sauce can be frozen.*

20 mins
Serves 2

Own invention
Mrs B. M. Hamilton, Perth

OEUFS A LA RUSSE

1 hard-boiled chopped egg, a little minced parsley, Parmesan cheese, 1 raw egg lightly beaten, a little milk, salt and pepper. Cream slightly together, then place on a *small* pancake (the shape of French pancakes), folding the two sides together and pressing edges slightly with a spoon to seal. Sprinkle with Parmesan cheese.
Place in fireproof dish and put in oven for a few minutes to get thoroughly hot.

Russians are fond of dishes with chopped fillings, i.e. mushrooms, shrimps, prawns, even small pieces of chicken, chopped up and added to the egg.

30 mins

Lady Zia Wernher from her father
the Grand Duke Michael of Russia
Mrs David Butter, Pitlochry

E APPLE CHUTNEY

2 lb. green apples
$1\frac{1}{2}$ lb. sugar
$\frac{1}{2}$ lb. sultanas
2 oz. currants
2 oz. preserved ginger
$\frac{1}{4}$ oz. cayenne pepper
1 pint vinegar
$\frac{1}{2}$ teaspoon salt
1 medium sized onion

Mince and mix all the ingredients together. Boil for 20-30 mins until it thickens.
Allow to stand for 24 hours before putting into pots.

1 hour
makes 4-5 lb.

Mrs E. Martin, Pitlochry

MRS CATNAP'S PICKLED DAMSONS

12 lb. damsons
12 lb. sugar
1 quart vinegar
¼ oz. cinnamon stick
¼ oz. cloves

Boil vinegar, sugar and spices together. Prick damsons well, and pour boiling liquor over the fruit. Allow to stand for 3 days. On the third day bring all to a simmer. Ready for eating when cold.

Brigadier Peter Young,
Captain-Generall of the Sealed Knot

E

APRICOT CHUTNEY

½ lb. dried apricots
¼ pint vinegar
½ lb. onions
½ lb. apples
½ lb. sultanas
½ lb. brown sugar
1 teaspoon ground ginger
2 teaspoons salt
1 teaspoon dry mustard

No cooking required. Mince apricots and leave to stand in vinegar overnight. Mince rest of ingredients and add to apricots, adding spices last.
Put into jars and seal down.

Mrs John Horsfall, Kinloch Rannoch

TOMATO CHUTNEY

8 lb. tomatoes
3 lb. apples
6 large onions
2 lb. brown sugar
3 pints vinegar
2 oz. salt

Boil sliced onions in vinegar. Add peeled and sliced tomatoes and apples. Add other ingredients.
Boil together until tender, and bottle when cool.

Mrs N. Jackson, Strathtay

E GOOSEBERRY BAR-LE-DUC

3 lb. ripe gooseberries
4 lb. sugar
½ pint brown vinegar

Top and tail gooseberries and put them into a pan with the vinegar and half the sugar. Cook for 20 mins, stirring frequently. Add the rest of the sugar and cook for another half hour or until the bar-le-duc is of syrupy consistency. Pot and cover immediately.
Delicious with meat or cheese.

15 mins *Mrs George Crerar, Pitlochry*

PICCALILLI

1 medium cauliflower
½ large cucumber
1 lb. shallots
½ lb. runner beans
½ lb. marrow
2 pints vinegar
1 tablespoon flour
1 oz. whole pickling spice
1 oz. mustard powder
½ lb. sugar
½ oz. ground ginger
½ oz. turmeric powder

Prepare and salt vegetables on dishes overnight. Boil the whole spice in a covered saucepan – not brass, copper or iron – with most of the vinegar for a few minutes.
Mix the other ingredients with the remaining cold vinegar to a smooth paste, add the strained spiced vinegar. Return to saucepan and boil for 15 mins on gentle heat, keeping well stirred.
Remove from heat, add vegetables (but not the salty liquid), and stir well. Allow to cool. Bottle in a large sweet jar if available.

Mrs W. Singleton, Logierait

VEGETABLES

DHAL CURRY

E

1½ pints water
1 teaspoon each of ground ginger, cumin, turmeric, salt
8 oz. red lentils
2 potatoes, diced
2 teaspoons curry powder (or more, according to taste)
2 tablespoons butter
1 large onion
1 green pepper
4 tomatoes, skinned and chopped
1 clove garlic, crushed
1 teaspoon ground ginger

Add the ground ginger, turmeric, cumin and salt to 1½ pints of cold water and bring to the boil. Stir in the lentils, bring to the boil again and simmer for 5 mins. Add the diced potatoes and continue cooking until the lentils are soft.
Heat butter in another pan, fry the chopped onion, pepper and tomatoes. Stir in the curry powder, extra ginger and garlic, and add to the lentil mixture. Cook for a further 5 to 10 mins and serve with rice and yoghurt.
I was brought up in the East End of Glasgow on lentil soup. Now I've progressed from the East End to the East with this lentil curry.

Serves 4 45 mins *John Cairney, Dunfermline*

CABBAGE CASSEROLE

E NF

1 round cabbage
2 oz. chopped bacon or ham
2 oz. butter
pinch of curry powder
seasoning

Soak cabbage in salted water to evict any insect lodgers. Trim off coarse outside leaves and cut bottom flat. Cut cabbage in a cross at the top so that it can open a little. Insert chopped bacon or ham between leaves, also butter, seasoning and curry powder. Put in well greased casserole and ensure that the lid fits firmly. Put into hot oven for 10 mins (gas mark 7), then reduce heat and cook until soft but still crisp (about ¾ - 1 hour). Drain off any excess liquid and serve in casserole.

Own invention

5 mins *Lady Kinnaird, Inchture*

RED CABBAGE AND APPLE

1 large red cabbage
1 lb. cooking apples
½ lb. onions
4 tablespoons butter or marg
2 cloves garlic, finely chopped
½ pint cheap red wine
2 tablespoons wine vinegar
½ teaspoon each of nutmeg, allspice, cinnamon, thyme, carroway seed, salt, black pepper
1 teaspoon grated orange rind
2 tablespoons brown sugar

Wash and shred cabbage in long strips, cook in covered pan for 5 mins. Slice and peel apples and onions. Put cabbage in large deep casserole in layers, alternating with apples and onions. Sprinkle each layer with garlic, spices, salt, pepper, orange rind, and sprinkle brown sugar over the top. Add wine and wine vinegar and a little hot water. Cover and simmer very slowly in a moderate oven till tender (about 1 hour).

Serve with chipolata sausages as main course and use afterwards as vegetable or salad. This is delicious with pork or ham.

Don't worry if you haven't got all the spices. Use what you have.

Serves 8-10 20 mins *Lady Stirling-Aird, Dunblane*

STUFFED MARROW

1 marrow
1 lb. minced beef
1 large onion
1 carrot
1 clove garlic
large tin tomatoes
1 cup breadcrumbs
salt, pepper
1 tablespoon oil

Halve marrow and remove pips with a metal spoon. Heat oil and add chopped onions, cook until transparent. Add grated carrot and beef, turn in pan for 3 mins and add tomatoes. Cook with lid on for 20 mins and then add seasoning with crushed clove of garlic. Add breadcrumbs until mixture is thick enough to form into a ball. Stuff each end of marrow, then join together and tie in a parcel. Rub marrow skin over with oil and bake in moderate oven. gas mark 5, for 1 hour. Serve with a fairly thick gravy. *Mrs Gerald Colin, Louth, Lincs*

E VEGETABLE MARROW IN DILL SAUCE

2 lb. tender vegetable marrow
1 heaped tablespoon salt
2 oz. lard
1½ oz. flour
½ teaspoon paprika-pepper
1 heaped tablespoon finely chopped or dried dill
1 level teaspoon sugar
1 gill sour cream

Peel young vegetable marrow, cut in two, scrape out inside. Cut marrow into strips and, putting it into a dish, sprinkle with salt. Leave to stand for ½ hour, drain off liquid, pressing marrow well between the hands to remove surplus juice.
Prepare roux in saucepan from the lard and flour, pull aside and add chopped dill and paprika-pepper. Add the squeezed-out marrow, add ¼ pint cold water and the sugar, stir, cover and allow to simmer for about ½ hour, stirring every now and then. Add the sour cream, cook for 5 more minutes and serve.

1 hour — Hungarian recipe
Serves 6-8 — *Mrs John Mackay, Pitlochry*

E NF BUTTERED LEEKS

Trim the leeks, leaving 1 inch of green. Slice fairly thinly, wash to remove grit, drain and plunge into boiling salted water off the heat. Leave 2 mins. Drain and plunge into cold water. Melt butter in saucepan – about ½ oz. for each 1 lb. leeks – and lightly toss till leeks are shiny. Add ground black pepper. Cover and cook gently, shaking occasionally, until tender but not mushy (up to 5 mins). Allow 1 lb. leeks for 2 people.

10 mins — *Mrs Atkinson-Clark, Tummelbridge*

FRIED ONION RINGS

Slice Spanish onions in $\frac{3}{8}$-inch slices. Dip in milk, then into flour which has been seasoned with salt and pepper. Drop into hot deep fat and fry until a medium brown. The onion rings will separate during the frying.
Serve at once while crisp.

Mrs R. S. Stewart-Wilson, Ballinluig

POTATO PANCAKES

3 medium potatoes
2 separated eggs
$1\frac{1}{2}$ tablespoons flour
$\frac{1}{2}$ teaspoon baking powder
salt, pepper

Grate raw potatoes and beat egg yolks. Mix together potatoes, flour, egg yolks, baking powder and salt and pepper. Beat egg whites and add to mixture.
Drop spoonfuls into hot fat and fry on both sides until brown.

Mrs Catternach and Miss A. M. Anderson,
Sunnybrae, Pitlochry

STOVIES

potatoes, sliced
1 large onion, sliced thinly
remains of stew
salt, pepper

Put potatoes and onion into a suitable pot, add remains of stew, cut up meat and gravy. Add a little water, and salt and pepper to taste.
Cook slowly until cooked.

Mrs S. Keith, Pitlochry

E F UPSIDE-DOWN VEGETABLE PIE

½ lb. mushrooms
2 medium onions, chopped
2 cups mashed potatoes (or dried potatoes)
oil or marg for frying
peas – fresh or tinned
2 cups white sauce
2 cups grated cheese
any cold meats (left over) for non-vegetarians, chopped
1 packet frozen mixed veg.
any extra veg, i.e. flowerettes of cauliflower (pre-cooked), marrow or 4-5 courgettes
2 boiled eggs
seasoning

Place mashed potato in ovenproof dish. Fry onions for 4 mins, add mushrooms, marrow and any cooked meat if desired. Fry for a good 10 mins.
Boil any frozen vegetables, mix all vegetables into the potato and season. Add chopped eggs.
Pour white sauce over the mixture and sprinkle with grated cheese. Cook in oven, 375° or gas mark 5, for approx. ½ hour.
This makes a very good vegetarian dish.

15 mins
Serves 4-5

Own invention
Mrs Peter Barr, Tenandry

E NF HOT CUCUMBER

Peel and dice a cucumber. Grease well a shallow ovenproof dish, place cucumber in with salt and pepper and a pinch of mixed herbs if liked. Cover with used butter papers and place in oven, 350° or gas mark 4, and cook until tender.
Delicious with meat or fish.

Serves 4

Mrs A. G. Godson, Headley, Hants

LEEKS AND TOMATO

Fry 1 chopped onion until golden brown. Add chopped leeks and some tomatoes, or tomato juice or tomato purée. Add a very little water, salt and pepper, and cook until tender.

Mrs Barbara Liddell, Pitlochry

PUDDINGS, CAKES, ETC.

E Very
NF Will never freeze

PRESERVING CHILDREN

1 large grassy field
1 or 2 small dogs
6 children
1 brook (with pebbles)

Mix children and dogs well together and place them in a field, stirring constantly. Pour brook over pebbles and add a few dozen minnows. Sprinkle field with flowers, spread over all a deep blue sky and bake in the sun. When brown, remove children. Set to cool in a bath, or better still a pool or ocean.

Time taken to make: all afternoon
Number of helpings: 6 plus dogs

South African W.R.I. recipe

Mrs J. Watters, Pitlochry

E CRUMBLE TOPPING FOR FRUIT

6 oz. flour
3 oz. marg
2 oz. castor sugar
a little demerara sugar

Mix together flour, marg and castor sugar. Press down on top of fruit and shake some demerara sugar over top. Cook in oven, 400° or gas mark 6, for 45 mins.
This makes an excellent topping for any fruit, e.g. gooseberries, blackcurrants, apple, rhubarb, bramble and apple. Do not have very much juice with fruit before covering with crumble mixture.
To freeze: I make 4 times this amount of crumble and freeze it in a polythene bag. It keeps well and you can put what you don't need back in the freezer for next time. It is very popular with children.

15 mins *Mrs Barbara Liddell, Pitlochry*

E CLOOTY DUMPLING

8 oz. self-raising flour
4 oz. marg
8 oz. sultanas or raisins
1 flat teaspoon baking soda
1 teaspoon mixed spice
2 good-sized carrots
1 good-sized apple
6 oz. sugar

Grate carrots and apple. Sieve flour and baking soda. Rub in marg, add remainder of ingredients. Bind with grated carrots and apple – no water or milk. Grate more carrots and apple if necessary.

Put in cloth, which must be scalded in boiling water and then rubbed with flour to keep the water out. Place in pot which has a plate at the bottom. Fill half way up with boiling water and steam for three hours.

Remember not to leave too much "slack" when tying the cloth, but leave enough room for it to swell. Do not put too much water in the pan; try not to have to add any water, but make sure it is boiling water if it has to be added. It may be dried off in a heated oven.

This is my wife's speciality and a birthday would not be the same without one.

Serves 8

Douglas Crawford, M.P. for Perth & East Perthshire, House of Commons

E NF LEMON DREAM

2 oz. butter
4 oz. castor sugar
2 eggs
1 oz. plain flour
juice and rind of 1 lemon
¼ pint milk

Cream butter and sugar together, beat in yolks of 2 eggs. Stir in 1 oz. plain flour, add juice and rind of 1 lemon. Add ¼ pint milk.

This mixture will then curdle. Whisk egg whites and fold in. Pour into well buttered oven dish. Stand in shallow pan of warm water and bake at gas mark 4.

20 mins

Serves 4

Lady Leechman, Edinburgh

E NURSE MASON'S STEAMED LEMON PUDDING

12 oz. self-raising flour
4 oz. marg } or 6 oz. suet
4 oz. lard }
1 cup granulated sugar
1 large lemon
pinch salt

Rub fat into flour, add salt. Grease a 7″ basin liberally. Mix pastry with a little cold water and roll out thickly. Line basin, reserving enough to make pastry lid.
Scrub lemon, and if very hard roll on a hard surface until soft. Place lemon in basin and add cup of sugar. Seal with pastry crust, cover with greased paper and foil, or scalded and floured pudding cloth. Steam for 2-2½ hours.
This pudding is beloved by all menfolk and womenfolk not dieting. The lemon remains whole, but when the pudding is cut the most delectable lemony goo oozes out.

15 mins
Serves 4-6

Mrs J. Duthie, Bridge of Cally

CHOCOLATE DREAM PUDDING

4 oz. flour
2 oz. sugar
2 teaspoons baking powder
¼ teaspoon salt
½ teacup milk
2 tablespoons cocoa
½ cup chopped nuts (optional)
1 teaspoon vanilla
2 tablespoons melted butter

sauce: 6 oz. soft brown sugar
2 tablespoons cocoa
2 teacups boiling water

Sift dry ingredients together, stir in nuts. Combine milk, butter and vanilla. Add liquids to dry mixture and blend thoroughly. Turn into greased shallow baking dish.
Mix brown sugar and cocoa for the sauce, and sprinkle over the batter in dish. Pour boiling water over mixture. Bake at 350° for 40-45 mins. During baking mixture separates into a rich cake with creamy fudge sauce. Serve hot.

New Zealand recipe
Lady Ogilvy-Wedderburn, Alyth

E NF CHOCOLATE FUDGE PUDDING

3 oz. self-raising flour
2 level tablespoons cocoa
pinch salt
4 oz. marg
4 oz. castor sugar
2 eggs
½ teaspoon vanilla essence
1-2 tablespoons milk to mix

Sauce:
4 oz. soft brown sugar
2 level tablespoons cocoa
½ pint hot water

Sift together flour, cocoa and salt and set aside. Cream marg and sugar till light. Beat eggs and essence lightly, and gradually add to creamed mixture. Add a little sifted flour with the last of the egg. Fold in remaining dry ingredients with enough milk to mix to a medium soft consistency. Put mixture into a well buttered 2-2½ pint pie dish and spread evenly.
Mix sauce as above, mixing well, and pour over cake mixture. Put pudding *at once* into centre of oven at 370° and bake for 40 mins. Can be served with fresh cream.
Very popular with children.

30 mins
Serves 6 *Mrs J. Falconer, Burnside Hotel, Pitlochry*

E SOUTHEND PUDDING

1½ oz. suet
3 oz. plain flour
1 egg
½ teacup milk
2 oz. demerara sugar
½ teaspoon baking powder
1 teaspoon ground ginger (optional)

Combine all ingredients. In buttered pie dish put any available fruit, or apricot jam, and turn mixture on to it. Bake in warm oven (335°, gas mark 3) for ¾ -1 hour.
This pudding can be adapted according to availability of fruit; stewed dried apricots work well. If using rhubarb, add chopped dates to the fruit, and include the ginger in the topping.

15 mins
Serves 4-6 *Mrs M. Collins, Rannoch*

E F MRS O'BRIEN'S GOOSEBERRY DREAM PUDDING

1 lb. gooseberries
8 oz. self-raising flour
6 oz. butter, or 3 oz. butter and 3 oz. marg
2 oz. demerara sugar

Cook gooseberries very slowly over low heat until soft. Strain, keeping juice to serve with pudding. Rub fat into flour until mixture is like crumbs. Mix in sugar with a knife.
Line a small deep cake tin with greaseproof paper. Sprinkle half flour mixture on bottom of tin and press down lightly. Spread strained gooseberries on to mixture and put rest of flour mixture on top of fruit. Press firmly.
Cook at 350° for approx 40 mins. Turn out just before serving and sprinkle with icing sugar. Serve hot with vanilla ice cream and/or cream, plus the juice from the gooseberries.
If freezing, freeze in the cake tin.

15 mins
Serves 6

Mrs Donald Dunlop, Dunalastair

E APPLE CAKE

apples
2 cups plain flour
2 teaspoons baking powder
¼ teaspoon salt
¾ cup milk
4 tablespoons butter
1 cup sugar
1 egg, unbeaten
½-1 teaspoon vanilla
cinnamon

This cake should be served as a dessert.
Sift flour and baking powder and salt together. Cream butter and sugar until light, add egg and beat well. Add flour alternately with the milk, then add vanilla.

Pour into 2 small greased layer tins. Pare and cut apples into eighths and arrange in circles or rows on the batter. Sprinkle thickly with cinnamon and sugar mixed together. Bake at 375° for 25 mins or until cooked. Top with whipped cream.

10 mins
Serves 6-8

Old Austrian recipe
Mrs Alastair Donald, Edinburgh

CHOCOLATE MARQUISE

Melt in the oven with a very little water $\frac{1}{2}$ lb. plain chocolate. In separate basin beat 4 egg yolks lightly and pass them through a sieve. Add sugar to taste and beat to a froth.

Add melted chocolate, beating all the time, by hand or with electric mixer at low speed. Add $\frac{1}{4}$ lb. unsalted butter, warmed but not melted.

Lastly add stiffly beaten egg whites and a little vanilla essence. This would not be necessary if vanilla sugar was used in place of plain sugar.

Turn mixture into mould which has been well brushed with oil of sweet almonds. Leave 24 hours, then turn out carefully. Cover with chantilly cream or serve cream separately.

This is a very rich and fattening dinner party pudding.

30 mins

Serves 6-8

Mrs P. B. Hay, Comrie

E LEMON AND CARAMEL MOUSSE

6 oz. sugar
$\frac{1}{4}$ pint water
plus
4 oz. sugar
$2\frac{1}{2}$ fl. oz. water

2 lemons
$\frac{1}{2}$ oz. gelatine
3 eggs
3 oz. sugar
$\frac{1}{4}$ pint cream

Make caramel, using 6 oz. sugar and $2\frac{1}{2}$ fl. oz. water. Add remaining $2\frac{1}{2}$ fl. oz. water. Heat until caramel has dissolved. Whisk 3 egg yolks with 3 oz. sugar over pan of hot water until thick. Continue whisking until cool.

Dissolve gelatine in juice of 2 lemons. Fold into mousse.

Whip cream and fold in. Fold in beaten egg whites and caramel.

To decorate: Use 4 oz. sugar and $2\frac{1}{2}$ fl. oz. water to make caramel. Pour on to greased tin. When cold crush into small pieces. Pipe mousse with whipped cream and decorate with caramel pieces.

Serves 6

Mrs Patrick Robinson, Hampton-in-Arden

E STRAWBERRY CLOUD

½ lb. strawberries
1 egg white
2-3 oz. icing sugar
1 tablespoon lemon juice

Hull strawberries. Do not wash unless absolutely necessary, and if so dry well on a towel. Mash roughly with fork.
Pour egg white into large bowl, or mixer bowl, whisk gently. Add strawberries and continue to whisk for 5 mins. at high speed in electric mixer, or 15-20 mins. with a rotary whisk. The mixture will rise miraculously up the bowl – which is why you need a large one. Whisk in lemon juice, spoon into serving bowl or individual dishes. Serve with digestive biscuits.
This is a good way of making a few strawberries go a long way.

10-20 mins
Serves 6-8

Mrs M. Mackenzie Smith, Blairgowrie

F KATARINA'S MERINGUE

Make and bake three layers of thin meringue, either rectangular or circular.

Fill as follows:
Place 4 egg yolks in a bain marie, and add 3 level tablespoons of sugar and 1 level tablespoon of plain flour. Mix well and cook slowly until mixture thickens. Add ¾ oz. unsalted butter. Allow to cool. Spread mixture on one layer of meringue and cover with fresh or frozen raspberries. Place second layer on top. Repeat the layering until the creamy mixture, the meringue layers and the raspberries are piled one on top of the other. Decorate the top layer of meringue with whipped cream and more raspberries.

30 mins (after making meringue)
Serves 10 to 12

Katarina Matic, distinguished Jugoslav cook
Lady Glen, Stanton, Broadway

E BLACK TREACLE SWEET

- $1\frac{1}{4}$ pints water
- 3 flat tablespoons arrowroot
- 5 dessertspoons black treacle

Mix arrowroot with a little of the cold water. Bring rest of the water to the boil, add treacle, stirring until boiling. Add arrowroot and stir for about 10 mins to cook.

Pour into wetted mould, or individual small moulds, and leave to set. Turn out or not, as preferred. Serve with whipped cream. Popular with anyone who likes the flavour of black treacle. The consistency can be altered by less or more water, and if liked softer it can be served in glasses.

Desiccated coconut makes an interesting texture if served in addition to the cream.

20 mins

Serves 5-6

This recipe was found in mother's handwriting on an odd scrap of paper

Mrs G. E. Borrowman, Dunkeld

E BONDEPIGE MED SLOR (Peasant Maid with Veil)

- 8 oz. breadcrumbs
- 3 oz. brown sugar
- 2 oz. butter or marg
- $1\frac{1}{2}$ lb. cooking apples
- lemon juice
- sugar to taste
- 2 oz. grated chocolate
- $\frac{1}{4}$ pint double cream

Mix crumbs and sugar together and fry in hot fat until crisp. Peel and core apples, cook to pulp in very little water, with a good squeeze of lemon juice and sugar to taste.

Put alternate layers of fried crumb mixture and apple pulp into glass dish, finishing with a layer of crumbs. When pudding is quite cold spread stiffly whipped cream on top and sprinkle with grated chocolate.

40 mins

Serves 8 to 10
(it is pretty solid)

Danish recipe

Mrs A. D. Cairncross, Perth

E ROOD FROOD

2 lb. raspberries
1 lb. red currants
3 oz. sago flour or
2 oz. potato flour
$1\frac{1}{2}$ pints water
1 lb. sugar
$\frac{1}{2}$ bottle claret

Put fruit with the water in *copper* pan and bring to boil. Strain through sieve and add 1 lb. sugar. When boiling thicken with 3 oz. sago flour or 2 oz. potato flour, which has already been mixed with $\frac{1}{2}$ bottle of claret. Set on ice and serve with cream.

This is the original recipe, but you can naturally use modern pans and equipment – and also water can be used instead of claret but the result will not be quite the same!

This was Queen Alexandra's own recipe
Mrs David Butter, Pitlochry

Serves 4-6

ALMOND MERINGUE PUDDING

4 egg whites
9 oz. castor sugar
vanilla essence
$\frac{1}{2}$ teaspoon vinegar
4 oz. ground almonds or
nut mix

Make meringue with egg whites and castor sugar. Add vinegar and vanilla essence, then add ground almonds or nuts.
Put in two sandwich tins, bake for 45 mins at gas mark 4. Sandwich together with cream. Fruit, e.g. pineapple pieces, can be added with cream.

15 mins
Serves 6

Mrs A. McDiarmid, Pitlochry

NF HONEY CREAM PUDDING

½ pint cream
2 tablespoons liquid honey
2 tablespoons malt whisky

Whip cream until very stiff. Add honey very slowly, stirring with wooden spoon. Then add whisky drop by drop, stirring again with wooden spoon.
Place in individual glasses and either use at once or leave in refrigerator.

10 mins
Serves 6 *Mrs M. Atkinson-Clark, Tummelbridge*

CHERRY CHEESE PIE

1 large or 2 smaller baked pastry cases
8 oz. cream cheese
6 oz. castor sugar
½ pint whipping cream
½ teaspoon vanilla essence
1 jar or tin (or more depending on size) cherry pie filling

Combine cheese, sugar and vanilla until smooth. Whip cream. Fold cream and cream cheese mixtures together. Put this into baked pastry case and cover with cherry pie filling.

Mrs Eileen Ward, Ponteland

F CHOCOLATE CHEESE CAKE

Base: 8 oz. chocolate coated digestive biscuits, crushed
4 oz. butter, melted

Add crushed biscuits to melted butter and line tin with loose base with mixture. Place in fridge.

Cheese mixture:

- 8 oz. cream cheese
- 4 oz. castor sugar
- 4 oz. plain chocolate
- 2 eggs, separated
- ½ pint double cream
- vanilla or rum
- crushed chocolate flake to decorate

Beat cream cheese, stir in half sugar and the flavouring. Melt chocolate over hot water, cool and beat in the cream cheese mixture, together with lightly beaten yolks. Beat whites of eggs until stiff and fold in remaining sugar. Fold this into cheese mixture. Finally fold in lightly whipped cream. Pour into lined tin and put into fridge to set.
When set decorate with crushed chocolate flake.

Serves 8-10 *Mrs Patrick Robinson, Hampton-in-Arden*

NF GRYFE GATEAU

- 4 oz. butter or soft marg
- 5½ oz. icing sugar
- 2 eggs
- 1 teaspoon vanilla essence
- 8 oz. crushed pineapple, drained
- 2 bananas
- 2 oz. flaked almonds
- 4 oz. double cream
- 8 oz. crushed ginger biscuits

Cream butter or marg with 4 oz. icing sugar. Beat in eggs and vanilla essence until mixture is creamy. In separate bowl combine drained pineapple, bananas finely sliced, and nuts. Fold in remainder of sugar. Whip cream and add to this mixture. Cover bottom of deep tin with ⅓ of crushed ginger biscuit crumbs. Pour creamed mixture on top. Add another layer of biscuit crumbs, then the fruit and cream mixture. Sprinkle remaining crumbs on top.
Chill in fridge overnight.

Serves 6-8 *Lady Taylor of Gryfe, Kilbarchan*

E NF RASPBERRY TART

Pâté sucrée:

- 8 oz. flour
- Pinch salt
- 4 oz. butter
- 2 egg yolks
- 2 oz. castor sugar

Make the pâté sucrée using above ingredients. Bake blind for 20 mins, but cover it with paper if it browns at the edges. Let the pastry shell cool.

Filling:

- $1\frac{1}{2}$ lb. raspberries
- 6 oz. sugar
- $\frac{1}{2}$ lb. red currants

Put ingredients in a pan, cook briefly so that the raspberries still retain their shape. Wild raspberries are particularly good but are not always available; however if you do find them you can use a lower proportion of red currants. If you use frozen fruit, thaw the berries out and retain any juices separately. Add it to the juice which is left from the cooked fruit.

Strain cooked fruit, put into the pastry shell and return to a moderate oven for about ten minutes.

Reduce juices to make a glaze, adding a tablespoon of red currant jelly. If you prepare this at about 4 o'clock in the afternoon it will still be crisp in the evening.

20 mins
Serves 6

Traditional French recipe
Colin H. Hamilton, Foss

E HONEY AND YOGHURT CHEESECAKE

- 5 oz. digestive biscuits, crushed
- $2\frac{1}{2}$ oz. butter
- 1 dessert spoon honey
- 5 oz. carton yoghurt
- 8 oz. packaged cream cheese
- 2 tablespoons honey
- $\frac{1}{2}$ teaspoon vanilla essence
- 1 teaspoon lemon rind
- 2 teaspoons gelatine
- 1 tablespoon water

Melt the butter and honey, stir in the crushed biscuits. Press on to the base of a 7″ flan tin.
Beat together yoghurt, cream cheese, honey, vanilla essence and lemon rind until smooth. Soften the gelatine in the water and dissolve over a pan of hot water. Fold it into the cream cheese mixture, pour on to the biscuit base and refrigerate.

20 mins
Serves 8 *John Cairney, Lassodie, near Dunfermline*

ALMOND DESSERT

- 8 oz. shortcrust pastry
- 4 oz. marg
- 4 oz. castor sugar
- 2 oz. ground rice
- 2 oz. ground almonds
- 1 egg
- 1 drop almond essence
- mincemeat

Line 7″ pie dish with pastry, bake blind, cool. Fill base with mincemeat. Cream marg and sugar, add egg and almond essence, ground almonds and ground rice. Mix well and spread mixture over mincemeat.
Bake in medium oven, 350°, for 45-50 mins until golden brown.

10-15 mins
Serves 6-8 *Mrs Shuttleworth, Craigard Hotel, Pitlochry*

E F CHOCOLATE FLUFF

- 4 eggs
- 3½ oz. castor sugar
- ¼ oz. gelatine
- 4 oz. drinking chocolate
- 1 teacup milk

Whisk egg yolks and sugar until thick and creamy. Dissolve gelatine in the milk, having soaked it in a little water first. Mix in the chocolate powder, and when cold add to the egg yolks and sugar. Whisk the egg whites until stiff and fold in.

20 -30 mins
Serves 5-6 A family recipe, handed down *Mrs C. Connell, Pitlochry*

NF BARMOUTH DESSERT

packet Barmouth biscuits
1 oz. marg
1½ oz. butter
2 oz. icing sugar
1 egg, whisked
1 lb. strawberries, fresh or frozen
½ pint double or whipping cream, sweetened

Crush biscuits. Melt the marg, mix well with crumbs. Place half this mixture in dessert dish. Cream butter with icing sugar and add whisked egg. Spread on top of crumb mixture. Put a layer of mashed strawberries on top, then half of the whipped cream. Then the remainder of crumb mixture, and the remainder of the whipped cream swirled on top. Decorate, if you wish, with a few halved strawberries.

15 mins
Serves 4

Mrs Duncan Menzies, Kenmore

 NF

SCOTCH WHISKY CHOCOLATE PUDDING

packet boudoir sponge fingers
¼ lb. butter
¼ lb. castor sugar
2 eggs
¼ lb. plain chocolate
2 tablespoons whisky
¼ pint double cream

Line 8″ loose based tin with sponge fingers. Cream butter and sugar together. Separate eggs, beat yolks into creamed butter and sugar. Melt chocolate and add to mixture, then beat in the whisky. Fold in stiffly beaten egg whites.
Pour into lined tin and refrigerate for 24 hours. Before serving top with whipped cream and decorate with chocolate curls.
A delicious party sweet but very rich.

25 mins
Serves 8

Mrs David Harley, Arthur Bell & Sons Ltd.

CHOCOLATE BISCUIT GATEAU

4 level dessertspoons cocoa
4 oz. marg
8 oz. castor sugar
1 egg
1 oz. chopped nuts
½ teaspoon vanilla flavouring
a little milk
6 oz. rich tea or petit beurre biscuits
cream to decorate

Well grease a small loaf-shaped tin or cake tin with marg. Melt the 4 oz. marg in a saucepan over low heat. Draw pan to one side, stir in the sugar and cocoa, previously mixed together. Beat egg and stir in, then stir the mixture over low heat until hot and cook it slowly for 10 mins, keeping it stirred and being careful not to let it boil. When nearly cooked stir in the chopped nuts and vanilla flavouring.

Have the biscuits ready to hand, and some milk in a small pie dish in which to dip them.

Pour a layer of the chocolate mixture into the base of the greased tin, then quickly add a layer of biscuits, dipping each one separately in milk and shaking off the surplus moisture. Meanwhile keep the chocolate mixture warm.

Continue in this way, filling the tin with alternate layers of chocolate mixture and biscuits, leaving enough chocolate for the top layer. Place a double thickness of greased paper on top and lightly weight this to keep the top level and the biscuits just covered with the chocolate. Leave until set, then dip the tin in hot water and turn out on to a dish. Decorate with cream.

Serves 12 *Mrs I. A. Duncan Millar, Aberfeldy*

E F CHOCOLATE ROULADE

4 eggs
3 oz. castor sugar
¼ pint cream
1½ oz. cocoa
2-3 tablespoons hot water
icing sugar

Separate eggs. Whisk yolks and sugar together, then add cocoa powder which has been mixed with hot water. Whisk whites of eggs stiffly and add chocolate mixture to whites. Line 12″ x 9″ tray with Bakewell paper. Bake in oven at gas no. 4 or 350° for 15 mins. Turn out and cover with greaseproof paper and damp cloth till cool. Fill with cream and roll up. Sprinkle with sugar.

20 mins
Serves 6 large helpings *Mrs J. Morison, Perth*

E F CARAMEL ICE CREAM

- 4 tablespoons granulated sugar
- 2 egg yolks
- ½ pint double cream

Put sugar and 2 tablespoons cold water into saucepan and caramelise it. Lower into sink (to avoid splashing) and add 4 tablespoons water. Simmer till combined.
Beat yolks, pour syrup into them slowly, beat until thick over a low heat. Allow to cool.
Whip cream and fold into caramel mixture.

Mrs John Horsfall, Kinloch Rannoch

♔ F CHOCOLATE ICE CREAM

- 2 oz. castor sugar
- 4 oz. plain chocolate
- ½ pint double cream
- 4 tablespoons cold water
- 3 large egg yolks

Dissolve sugar in water. Boil for about 2-3 mins. Break chocolate into liquidiser. Pour in hot syrup and blend until chocolate is melted. Drop in the yolks, blend until slightly paler in colour. Beat cream until beginning to thicken. Fold into the chocolate mixture.
Pour into 6-8 small pots and freeze. Bring out 5-10 mins before serving.

20 mins
Serves 6-8 *Mrs A. Henderson, Aberfeldy*

GIN SORBET

2 x 16 oz. tins grapefruit segments
3 oz. sugar
4 fl. oz. gin

Empty juice from both tins into a saucepan, add enough water to make 1½ cups of liquid. Add sugar, boil for 5 mins until a syrup forms. Cool. Add grapefruit segments and gin, liquidise. Put the sorbet in deep freeze for 1 hour. Stir thoroughly, then put it back in the freezer to solidify – it never becomes completely solid.
Remove from freezer and put in fridge one hour before it is needed.

15 minutes
Serves 6-8

Mrs R. Walls, Bankfoot

BISCUIT TORTONI

¾ pint double cream
¼ pint single cream
pinch salt
3 fl. oz. brown sherry
2 oz. icing sugar
12 macaroon biscuits or packet small macaroons

Whip cream with sugar and salt until firm but not stiff. Spoon into a 9″ tin, previously chilled. Cover with foil and nearly freeze solid. Crush macaroons in a plastic bag and set aside about one-third of them. Break up ice cream into bowl, blend in sherry and two-thirds of macaroon crumbs. Return to tin and put back in freezer until hard and firm.
To serve remove from tin, coat with remaining macaroon crumbs and decorate with glacé cherries.

15 mins
Serves 6

Mrs John H. Christie, Glenfarg

E F CHOCOLATE, RUM AND RAISIN ICE CREAM

½ pint double cream
2 eggs
2 oz. castor sugar
2 oz. seedless raisins
2 oz. plain chocolate
rum

Cover raisins with rum and soak overnight. Cream egg yolks and sugar, whip cream and fold in. Whip egg whites until stiff and fold in, then add rum, raisins and chopped chocolate. Line oblong tin with foil and put in mixture, seal and freeze. Turn out and serve straight from the freezer.

15 mins
Serves 4-6

Mrs R. Rorie, Laide

FRUIT CAKE

1 breakfast cup cold water
1 breakfast cup sugar
1 lb. mixed fruit
2 teaspoons mixed spice
2½ cups flour
2 whole eggs
4 oz. marg
2 teaspoons soda bicarbonate

Put into saucepan water, sugar, fruit and marg. Bring to boil and let it froth. Allow to cool. Add 2 whole eggs, 2½ cups sifted flour, mixed spice and the soda bicarbonate. Mix well.
Line loose bottomed 7-inch tin with tin foil. Spoon in mixture and cook in pre-heated oven, gas mark 4, for approx. 2 hours. After 1 hour place a paper loosely on the top to prevent burning. When cooked allow it to cool in the tin and stand it on a rack.

This is so easy, and quite delicious with a slightly spicy gingery flavour. It keeps for weeks in a tin.

15 mins

Lady Stirling-Aird, Dunblane

♔ F CHOCOLATE LAYER CAKE

5 oz. self-raising flour
1 oz. cocoa powder
6 oz. butter or marg
1 teaspoon vanilla essence
4 oz. plain chocolate
3 tablespoons boiling water
4 large eggs

Break chocolate into small saucepan and add boiling water. Stir to melt. Cream butter and sugar, add chocolate mixture. Add essence. Separate eggs, beat yolks and add gently after the flour (sifted) and chocolate. Spoon into two greased and lined 8″ spongecake tins, spread level. Place in centre of moderate oven, 355° or gas mark 4, for 30 mins. Cool for 5 mins in tins. Fill with butter cream and cover with chocolate icing.

Cook at Holme Rose

10 mins

Serves 12 *The Rt. Hon. Lord Campbell of Croy, M.C., Cawdor*

E F GRANNIE'S DRIPPING CAKE

5 oz. *beef* dripping
6 oz. brown sugar
2 eggs
½ teaspoon mixed spice
8 oz. plain flour, sprinkled with baking powder
grated rind of 1 lemon
4 oz. currants
4 oz. sultanas
2 oz. candied peel
2 oz. glacé cherries

Mix dripping and sugar together. Beat eggs, add to this mixture and beat well. Add flour, previously combined with spice. Then add fruit. A little milk may be necessary to make a really wet mixture.

Bake in moderate oven for 1½ hours.

I used to make this, and also bread, when I was eight years old, in an old-fashioned Derbyshire kitchen with an open range. The bread was put along the fender to rise.

My great grandmother
Mid-nineteenth century

30 mins

Medium sized cake *The Marchioness of Aberdeen and Temair, Haddo House, Aberdeen*

E

CHRISTMAS CAKE

- $1\frac{1}{2}$ lb. mixed dried fruit (sultanas, currants, raisins)
- $\frac{1}{4}$ lb. chopped candied peel
- 4 oz. quartered glacé cherries
- 2 oz. shredded almonds or walnuts
- 10 oz. plain flour
- 1 teaspoon baking powder
- 1 teaspoon mixed spice
- 1 dessertspoon cocoa
- $\frac{1}{2}$ lb. butter
- $\frac{1}{2}$ lb. dark brown sugar
- 1 tablespoon black treacle
- 1 dessertspoon coffee essence
- large pinch salt
- grated rind of 1 orange
- 1 gill brandy
- 4 eggs
- few drops almond essence

Three days before making cake prepare the mixed dried fruit and place in a screw topped jar. Sprinkle over the brandy, cover closely and leave for 3 days, shaking at intervals – and resisting the urge to sniff and taste!

Line 8-inch cake tin with double thickness of greaseproof paper. Add cherries, peel and nuts to soaked fruit. Sieve flour, baking powder, cocoa, salt and spice. Cream butter with grated rind, add sugar and cream again very thoroughly. Beat in treacle, coffee essence and then 4 eggs, beating mixture well between each addition.

Fold in half the flour very lightly, then add soaked fruit, etc. and remaining flour alternately, including any liquid not absorbed by fruit. Add almond essence.

Put mixture into cake tin, hollowing the centre slightly. Bake at 300° for first 2 hours, reduce to 275° for further $1\frac{1}{2}$ hours. This makes $3\frac{1}{2}$ hours altogether. Leave cake in tin in oven with heat off for a further $\frac{1}{2}$ hour. *Keeps well in a tin for at least* 6 *weeks.*

Mrs J. Lamb, Pitlochry

E

COFFEE AND WALNUT SPONGE CAKE

6 oz. soft marg
6 oz. castor sugar
6 oz. self-raising flour
2 oz. walnut crumbs
1 level teaspoon baking powder
3 eggs
1 level teaspoon instant coffee in 2 tablespoons cold water

N.B. Granulated sugar can be made into castor sugar by liquidising for ½ minute. Walnut halves can also be broken down to crumbs by using a liquidiser.

Grease and flour 2 x 8-inch sandwich tins, pre-heat oven to 350°. Place all ingredients in large bowl and mix, using an electric hand mixer, at slowest speed for 1-2 mins.
Bake for 30 mins till firm to touch.
To fill: Mix together to a creamy consistency 6 oz. icing sugar, 1½ oz. soft marg, 1 level teaspoon instant coffee in 2 dessertspoons cold water. Sandwich sponges together with half the filling. Spread remaining icing on top and decorate with walnut halves.

Only minutes to make
Serves 12

Mrs John Brydone, Pitlochry

E F

GRANNY'S LEMON CAKE

4 oz. soft marg
4 oz. castor sugar
2 eggs
1 tablespoon lemon curd
rind of ½ lemon
5 oz. self-raising flour

Beat marg and sugar, add eggs one at a time, beating well between each one. Mix in lemon curd. Fold in flour. Bake in a lined 7″ x 3″ tin for ½ hour at gas mark 4, and for 15 mins at gas mark 3.
While the cake is baking dissolve 3 tablespoons granulated sugar with the juice of 1 lemon and the rind of half a lemon. Pour over cake while still hot in the tin.
Leave to cool.
20 mins
Serves at least 8

Lady Fraser, Dunblane

E CAKES – TWO FOR TEA

$\frac{1}{2}$ lb. short crust pastry (1 packet prepared short pastry will suffice) makes:

(a) **Border Tart**. Line a 7″ sponge tin with pastry and fill with fruit filling. Decorate with small "islands" of pastry.

Filling: 2 oz. soft brown sugar
2 oz. marg
yolk of 1 egg
teacup of raisins, adding a few chopped cherries

Melt marg over low heat, add sugar and raisins. Remove from heat and fold in yolk of egg and cherries. When cool spread over pastry case.

(b) **Macaroons**. Cut out pastry circles to cover a 9-cup bun tray.

Filling: 2 oz. castor sugar
2 oz. desiccated coconut
$\frac{1}{2}$ teaspoon almond essence
a little jam or jelly

Whisk white of the egg till stiff, then fold in sugar and coconut. Spoon a little jam or jelly into each pastry base, then a spoonful of filling.

Bake both the above in moderate oven, 350°, the Border Tart above centre and the Macaroons near the bottom of the oven, for approx. 40-45 mins till golden brown. When cold the "islands" of pastry on the Tart may be covered with a blob of icing.

The above originated from a friend in wartime, when the precious egg ration had to be stretched as far as possible. "Two for the price of one" seemed a bargain!

approx 30 mins
8 pieces from tart,
and 9 macaroons

Miss Winifred Ednie, Pitlochry

F

CHOCOLATE CAKE

Sieve: 6 oz. plain flour
2 oz. cocoa
1 level teaspoon soda bicarbonate
½ level teaspoon salt

10 oz. castor sugar
4 oz. marg
2 large eggs
¼ pint sour milk

This makes 2x7½-inch to 8-inch cakes, or 3 smaller 5½-inch across.
Line tins with Bakewell kitchen parchment.
Cream sugar and marg, mix all together until smooth batter.
Divide into tins and cook at 350° for 25-30 mins. Leave in tins 10 mins before turning out.
Filling and top: 1½ oz. marg., 2 tablespoons water and 2 oz. castor sugar. Stir together until sugar is dissolved, then stir in 3 oz. castor sugar and 1 oz. cocoa sieved together. Spread quickly in middle and on top before it becomes fudge.

Miss Diana Dixon, J.P., Louth, Lincs.

E F

AMERICAN SWEET PASTRY

This will keep up to 6 months in a fridge.
Cream together 2 oz. lard with 2 oz. marg. Dissolve 1 level tablespoon of sugar with 1 level tablespoon boiling water, cool. Mix into the creamed lard and marg. Finally work in 6 oz. plain flour.
Roll out and cut with pastry cutter to fit into tart cases. Cook at 350° for 25 mins.
This pastry never fails and is excellent for small tart cases.

40 mins
makes 18 small tart cases

Mrs Hastie Smith, Comrie

F AUSTRALIAN FRUIT CAKE

8 oz. sugar
1 lb. mixed dried fruit
1 level teaspoon nutmeg
1 level teaspoon bicarbonate of soda
4 oz. self-raising flour
4 oz. plain flour
4 oz. butter or marg
2 eggs
4 oz. crushed pineapple
½ pint or less pineapple juice and water
pinch salt

Put sugar, water, fruit, pineapple, nutmeg, bicarbonate of soda and marg into saucepan and heat gently till marg melts. Bring to boil and cook for 1 minute. *Allow to become quite cold.* Put eggs in large basin and beat slightly with wooden spoon. Add cold fruit mixture. Beat in sifted flour and pinch of salt gradually, and mix till mixture is thoroughly blended in.

Put in greased and lined 8-inch tin and bake at 350°, gas mark 4, for 1 to 1½ hours till firm and skewer comes out clean when tested.

Quick to make

Mrs Charles Tennant, Rosemount

E F SWEET OVEN SCONES

1 lb. plain flour
4 oz. lard
4 oz. sugar
2 teaspoons cream of tartar
1 teaspoon bicarbonate of soda
salt
milk
¼ lb. currants can be added to these quantities if a currant scone is required

Sift salt with flour, rub in lard. Add sugar, and currants if used, cream of tartar and bicarbonate of soda. Using a knife mix with milk to a sticky mixture, then roll out on a well floured board. Bake in the bottom of a hot oven, turn over when half cooked. *These scones should not be over baked. They are remarkably good to eat for several days afterwards and do not become dry and stale.*

Great great grandmother's recipe, before 1860

Mrs M. H. Bruges, Dunkeld

ECONOMICAL USE OF FIVE EGGS

Meringues (using 5 whites):

5 egg whites
9 oz. castor sugar
pinch of salt
pinch of cream of tartar

Place egg whites in bowl with salt and cream of tartar, whisk until stiff. Fold in sugar gradually. Pile in small spoonfuls on baking sheet lined with greaseproof paper. Cook in very slow oven for approx. 2 hours. Remove from paper, cool and store in airtight tin.

Chocolate gateau (using 5 yolks):

5 egg yolks
5 tablespoons castor sugar
5 tablespoons water
4 tablespoons self-raising flour
1 tablespoon cocoa
½ teaspoon baking powder
a little boiling water – 1 tablespoon at the most
whipped cream
grated chocolate
toasted almonds

Sieve together flour, cocoa and baking powder. Whisk together yolks, sugar and water until very thick and creamy. Quickly fold in dry ingredients. Stir in boiling water and pour into 2 7-inch sandwich tins. Bake approx. 10 mins at 400°. When cold sandwich together with whipped cream and spread cream on top. Decorate with grated chocolate and toasted almonds. This sponge should be used within 3-4 days of baking.

I have an Aga and make the two recipes simultaneously, the sponges in the top oven and the meringues in the lower.

30 mins
20 meringues
8 portions gateau

Mrs Olive Holden, Strathtay

♔ F "BLACK DOG" GINGERBREAD

8 oz. sugar
8 oz. butter
1 lb. black treacle

Melt these together in pan over low heat.

Meanwhile sieve into large bowl:

1 lb. plain flour
2 teaspoons ground ginger
2 teaspoons mixed spice
1 teaspoon baking soda

Add ¼ pint milk to the butter and treacle mixture and mix well. Make a well in the middle of the dry ingredients and pour mixture in, stirring with a wooden spoon. Beat 2 eggs and add to mixture. Beat all together well and bake in a moderate oven, 350° for 1 hour. Makes 3 lb. gingerbread.
Sultanas may be added if wished.

Mrs Stewart-Stevens, Moulin

GINGER BREAD

2 lb. flour
1 lb. demerara sugar
1 pint milk
2 teaspoons ground ginger
2 teaspoons mixed spice
2 teaspoons bicarbonate of soda
1 lb. marg
1 lb. black treacle
4 eggs

Melt marg with treacle and sugar. Do not boil. Add part of the milk. Stir melted treacle, etc. into the dry ingredients and add the rest of the milk. Mix well. Add beaten eggs. Bake in a slow oven for 2 hours.
These amounts make three 2-pound loaves.
Used for all hill lunches, especially on 12th August.

Mrs I. A. Duncan Millar, Aberfeldy

MOIST FRUIT GINGER CAKE

8 oz. self-raising flour
4 oz. treacle
4 oz. golden syrup
3 oz. brown sugar
4 oz. marg
1 large egg
1 cup milk
½ teaspoon bicarbonate of soda
1 teaspoon mixed spice
2 teaspoons ground ginger
½ lb. raisins

Mix all dry ingredients together. Melt marg, treacle, syrup and sugar in milk. When dissolved and well mixed pour in beaten egg.
Mix with dry ingredients and pour into a well buttered cake tin. Bake in moderate oven, 350°, for 1½ hours.

Mrs Lilian Grant, Pitlochry

E F SOFT BLACK GINGERBREAD

8 oz. self-raising flour
4 oz. brown sugar
4 oz. butter or marg
8 oz. treacle
1 cup milk
1 teaspoon ground ginger
1 teaspoon allspice
1 egg
fruit and peel if liked

Sift dry ingredients. Melt butter or marg, sugar and treacle. Cool slightly and beat in milk and egg. Pour into dry ingredients, mixing well to make a liquid pouring mixture. Grease and line 7″ tin and pour mixture in. Bake slowly (1-1½ hours) at gas mark 3. It is even better if baked for much longer in a double tin.
This cake keeps very well and grows moister and moister the longer it is kept. It is delicious spread with butter.
A very good chocolate cake can be made by substituting syrup for treacle, and 1 oz. cocoa powder for 1 oz. flour.

15 mins
Serves 10-12

Mrs E. F. Aglen, Ballintuim

E F BUTTERSCOTCH SQUARES

4 oz. butter
10 oz. soft brown sugar
2 eggs
6 oz. self-raising flour
2 teaspoons vanilla essence
2 oz. chopped walnuts

Melt butter and soft brown sugar together and beat in 2 eggs. Add flour, chopped walnuts and vanilla essence. Put into greased swiss roll tin and bake at gas mark 4 for 25-30 mins. Cut while warm.

10 mins

Serves 12

Recipe supplied by Miss Muriel Lamond, cateress

Mrs D. E. Foster, Ardvreck School, Crieff

E PORTKNOCKIE SHORTBREAD

12 oz. plain flour
5 oz. rice flour
8 oz. marg
4 oz. butter
5 oz. castor sugar

Cream fat and sugar till white and soft. Sieve in flour and mix well. Divide mixture into four 7″-8″ round tins. Smooth, crimp edges and prick with a fork.
Bake at 340° for 20-25 mins. until golden brown. Cut immediately, but leave for 10 minutes before lifting on to a wire tray.

10 minutes

Makes 48 pieces

Very old family recipe

Mrs P. T. MacLellan, Rannoch

PARKINS

1 lb. flour
1 lb. oatmeal
¾ lb. sugar
¾ lb. syrup, or
  ½ lb. syrup and
  ¼ lb. treacle

½ lb. marg
2 eggs
3 teaspoons baking soda
2 teaspoons ground ginger
2 teaspoons cinnamon
1 teaspoon mixed spice

Mix dry ingredients together and rub in marg. Beat eggs and mix with syrup, add to dry ingredients and knead to a stiff dough.
Break off small pieces and roll in palms of hands till like marbles. Bake on greased tins in moderate oven, gas mark 3, till dark brown.

Miss C. Marshall, Pitlochry

E F

PLUM BREAD

½ lb. marg
½ lb. sugar
1 lb. mixed dried fruit

2 eggs
1 tablespoon syrup
18 tablespoons self-raising flour

Put fruit in a saucepan and cover with water. Simmer for a few mins. Allow to cool.
Rub fat into flour. Add sugar, syrup and beaten eggs. Add fruit and enough liquid to make a smooth mixture.
Bake in moderate oven for about 2 hours, the mixture divided into 2 bread tins. Slice, butter and eat with cheese.

Mrs N. Jackson, Strathtay

E NF BANANA BREAD

4 oz. margarine
8½ oz. flour
8½ oz. sugar
1 teaspoon baking powder
½ teaspoon salt
4 ripe bananas, mashed
2 eggs
1 teaspoon vanilla essence
2 oz. chopped nuts (optional)

Cream margarine and sugar, add eggs and vanilla. Mash bananas well, and add with nuts. Fold in sifted dry ingredients. The mixture will be stiff. Pour into well greased loaf tin and bake at 375° for 1¼ hours.

Mrs T. Rossaak, Johannesburg

E F A VERY HEALTHY BROWN LOAF

6 cups wholewheat flour
1 cup wheatgerm
1 cup wheat bran (or porage oats)
1 cup crushed wheat
1 cup sunflower seed
½ cup sesame seed
½ cup linseed seed
1 tablespoon salt

1. Mix all dry ingredients in large bowl.
2. Mix one cake yeast (20 grammes) with 4 teaspoons castor sugar. If using dried yeast mix 3 dessertspoons dried yeast in a jug with ⅔ cup hot water (hand hot) with 4 teaspoons castor sugar, and whisk with fork till creamy. It won't entirely dissolve and should form a gooey mass at the bottom of the jug. Cover and keep warm 3 to 5 minutes. It should now be frothing vigorously.
3. In another jug mix one tablespoon of honey and one dessertspoon of molasses (from Health Shop – de-sulphured). Mix with at least 2 pints hot water.
4. Add yeast mix to this, and stir into dry ingredients as quickly and thoroughly as possible. It should be quite wet. Put straight into greased tins and leave to rise for at least one hour. Bake at 375° for 50 mins. Turn out on to wire rack at once.

Ingredients can be varied. If sunflower seed or any other ingredients are left out, just substitute more flour.

Mrs T. Rossaak, Johannesburg

E F WHOLEMEAL BREAD

- 1½ lb. 100% compost grown wholemeal flour
- ½ oz. reconstituted dried yeast
- about ¾ pint warm water
- 1 level tablespoon sea salt
- 1 heaped tablespoon molasses

Mix half the flour with the water. Add the yeast, which has been previously mixed with a little water and has frothed, to the mixture. Leave covered with a clean cloth for 10 mins.

Add salt and molasses, stirring well. Add remaining flour, stir well again. Leave in a well-oiled tin, covered with a cloth, in a warm place to rise.

Bake in a pre-heated oven, gas mark 8, on the middle shelf for 15 mins, then at mark 7 for a further 30 mins. Turn out on to rack to cool.

I never knead, so that the bread has an attractively coarse texture. These quantities make a 2lb. loaf. The molasses are essential to the darker colour and moistness and flavour.

Gabriel Woolf, London

F APRICOT TEA BREAD

Grease 2x1-pound loaf tins. Cut 1 lb. dried apricots into small pieces and stew in ¾ pint of water. Add 2 more tablespoons of water, ¾ lb. castor sugar, 6 oz. lard, 1 level teaspoon cinnamon, 1 level teaspoon ground cloves, 1 level teaspoon nutmeg and 1 level teaspoon salt. Cook together for 3 mins and allow to cool.

Add 2 beaten eggs and 1 lb. self-raising flour. Divide between the 2 tins and bake in moderate oven, gas mark 4 or 360° for about an hour.

This is delicious and keeps well.

30 mins *Mrs W. G. Gordon, Blair Atholl*

E F "NO MIXING BOWL" FRUIT LOAF

Melt, in a large saucepan: 3 oz. marg, 1 cup sultanas or mixed fruit, 1 cup granulated sugar, 1 cup water, 1 teaspoon bicarbonate of soda.
Boil gently for 10 minutes, leave to cool for 5-10 mins. Add 1 beaten egg and 2 cups self-raising flour. Mix well. Line a loaf tin with butter paper and pour mixture in. Bake at 425° for 30-40 mins.
These quantities will make 2 small 7-inch loaves, or 1 large.

Mrs Rabiash, wife of chef at Fisher's Hotel, Pitlochry

FLORENTINE BISCUITS

3 oz. marg
4 tablespoons milk
squeeze lemon juice
2 oz. flaked almonds
4 oz. icing sugar
$1\frac{1}{2}$ oz. plain flour
5 oz. mixed dried fruit
4 oz. cooking chocolate

Melt marg in pan, add icing sugar. Dissolve, add milk and stir. Add flour gradually, add lemon juice, fruit and nuts. Line baking tray with Bakewell paper and place teaspoons of mixture on it.
Bake at 375° for 10 mins. Allow to cool on wire tray. Melt chocolate and coat the back of the biscuits.

30 mins *The Dowager Countess of Mansfield, Perth*

E F QUICK AND ECONOMICAL SHORTBREAD

8 oz. plain flour
4 oz. soft marg
2 oz. sugar

Either in mixer bowl, or with a fork, blend the marg and sugar. Add the flour, all at once or in two lots, and mix just enough to become like breadcrumbs.
Using a tin about 7″ x 10″, spread into tin and smooth out, then press down with the flat of the hand and finally bang all over with the fist. Smooth edges with a knife and mark out into fingers.
Bake at 300° for approx. 40 mins. When cooked, re-cut over original marks, sprinkle with castor sugar and take out very carefully with a fish slice. Cool on a wire tray.
This shortbread can be cooked in a hotter oven for a shorter time, but cooking it at 300° for 40 mins produces a very good light coloured shortbread, and is very easy to do on the top shelves while you are cooking a stew or something below. *It is very good with fruit fools and other puddings, as well as for tea. Keeps well in tin.*

15 mins *Mrs C. Findlay, Killiecrankie*

E NF OATCAKES

8 oz. self-raising flour
8 oz. medium oatmeal
1 teaspoon salt
5 oz. marg (not soft variety)
2 oz. syrup
4 tablespoons hot water

Rub marg into oatmeal, salt and sifted flour. Dissolve syrup in hot water and pour on dry ingredients. Mix to a firm moist dough. Take a large handful and roll out thinly on floured board. Using approx. 7-inch round plate or flan base cut into a circle and then divide into 4 quarters.
Bake at 360°, gas mark 4, for 15-20 mins.

45 mins
20 oatcakes *Mrs C. W. Grant, Pitlochry*

MINCEMEAT

1½ lb. stoned raisins
1½ lb. currants
1½ lb. suet
3 lb. brown sugar
4½ oz. candied peel
3 tablespoons marmalade
5 apples
5 lemons – juice and rind
1½ teaspoons brandy

Peel and chop the apples, grate the lemon rinds. Mix all together and moisten with the brandy.
This is an old family recipe which is very juicy, and keeps well.

20 mins

Craigivar, Aberdeen
1893

Mrs T. S. Drew, Coupar Angus

E F

UNCOOKED JAM

1¼ lb. strawberries or raspberries
2 lb. castor sugar
½ bottle Certo
2 tablespoons lemon juice

Crush the fruit, add sugar. Leave to stand for 1 hour or more in warm kitchen while sugar dissolves in the fruit, stirring occasionally.
Add lemon juice and Certo, combine well, and stir for 2 mins.
Pour into small jars, leaving ½″ head room. Cover with foil.
Leave in warm kitchen a further 48 hours, then freeze.
These quantities make about 3½ lb. and will keep up to 6 months in freezer. This tastes better than any cooked jam, and is equally good with loganberries or blackberries.

Mrs A. D. Cairncross, Perth

MARMALADE

E

3 lb. Seville oranges
3 sweet oranges
2 lemons
11 pints water
13 lb. sugar

Wash fruit, skin and shred skins of fruit. Remove pips and place them in small pan with enough water to cover them. Squeeze juice from fruit into jelly pan. Mince remainder of fruit and add to shredded skins and juice in jelly pan, add water. Steep pulp and pips separately for 2 nights.
Boil each lot for 45 mins, strain juice from pips into jelly pan. Cool and add sugar, boil again for 30 mins.
Makes about 25 lbs.

Note re freezing: As the marmalade season is limited, I have found it very useful to freeze batches of pulp. To do this the pips are added to pulp before freezing. When making the marmalade add bulk of measured water and proceed as above.

Mrs K. MacVicar, Kenmore

LEMON CURD

$\frac{1}{4}$ lb. butter
$\frac{1}{2}$ lb. sugar
3 lemons
3 eggs

Melt butter. Add sugar, juice and finely grated rind of lemons. Allow to stand for a few minutes. Add beaten eggs, and cook in double pan till thick.
Do *not* allow to boil.

Miss F. Mackinnon, Pitlochry

PEACH AND RASPBERRY MARMALADE

I never tire of marmalade and this one makes a pleasant change for summer. I always look forward to it being made in July, when the Perthshire raspberries are so readily available and the Italian cling peaches are at their best.

Skin 3½ lb. peaches by dipping them into boiling water for 10 seconds and then into cold water, after which the skins will easily rub off. Cut into halves and remove the stones. Crack these and remove the kernels. Put peaches and 1 lb. fresh raspberries, and the kernels in a muslin bag, into preserving pan, and cook very gently until tender. This should take about 40 mins. Add 3 lbs. preserving sugar and stir until dissolved. Add the juice of a lemon and boil fairly briskly for 10-12 mins. Test for setting.

It is most important to keep a constant watch that the marmalade never burns as there is very little water content in this process. When ready, rest for 10 mins and pot in sterilised jars. These quantities should yield about 6 lbs.

2 hours *Basil Death, Calvine*

E ROWAN JELLY

Just cover the berries with water, boil until they are tender. Empty into jelly bag and leave to drip overnight.

Allow 1 lb. sugar to 1 pint liquid and boil slowly until sugar dissolves. Then boil fast until jelly sets when tested in saucer. Store as for jam.

This is delicious with venison or mutton. It is an old family recipe and keeps well. It is very important that the berries are completely strained as the berry itself is not edible.

Mrs Angus Stroyan, Killin

ATHOLE BROSE

Strain a handful of oatmeal through a fine sieve into a basin, and mix with cold water till the consistency of a thick paste. Be careful not to make it too watery. Add 4 dessertspoons of run honey to 4 sherry glasses of the sieved oatmeal. Stir well together and put into a quart bottle. Fill up with whisky. Shake well before serving.

Can be drunk at once, or kept indefinitely if well corked and sealed. The bottle should be kept standing upright. Some ladies like a little cream added to it immediately before serving.

His Grace the Duke of Atholl, Blair Atholl

RASPBERRY CORDIAL

2½ lb. raspberries — 1 pint white vinegar

Bring raspberries to the boil, pour on vinegar and bruise raspberries with a wooden spoon.

Allow to stand for a few days. Cover well in order not to attract flies.

Strain through a jelly bag, add ½ lb. sugar to each breakfast cup of juice. Boil for 5 mins. Skim, bottle when cool.

This is delicious poured undiluted over ice cream, or is excellent used as a hot drink when one has a cold. Children like it as an iced drink.

Mrs Maitland-Smith, Dunkeld

E ANNANDALE LIQUEUR

Mix ½ lb. fine oatmeal into a paste with ½ pint cold water, using a silver spoon. When well blended stir in a bottle of whisky and leave overnight. Strain and discard the oatmeal. Add the juice of 2 lemons, 6 oz. castor sugar and half a section of honey or equivalent of liquid heather honey. Finally add ½ pint cream and keep tightly corked until required.

Mrs Mary C. Annandale, Perth

NF

CLARET CUP

To each bottle of Burgundy or claret add 1 glass of sherry and 1 liqueur glass of orange Curaçao, lemon peel cut very thin, and 2 tablespoons castor sugar to each bottle used.
Let this remain a short time on ice. Just before serving add 2 bottles of soda water (splits). Decorate with fresh mint.

5 mins *Dr. Kenneth Ireland, O.B.E., Pitlochry*

E

LEMON OR ORANGE SQUASH

6 lemons or 6 oranges
1 oz. citric acid
1 oz. tartaric acid
2 oz. Epsom salts
4 lb. sugar
10 breakfast cups boiling water

Grate lemons or oranges into heatproof basin. Squeeze juice from fruit, add with sugar, salts and acids. Add boiling water and stir every time you pass it for 24 hours.
Strain and bottle. Dilute to taste. Makes about 5 pints.

30 mins *Mrs J. Morris Wood, Perth*

CITRUS DRINK

1 lemon, peeled
1 orange, peeled
1 egg, unbroken
½ pint cold water
3 tablespoons sugar
few ice cubes

Put all ingredients in liquidiser, turn on full speed for 2 mins. Strain into glasses and drink immediately.

Mrs Catternach and Miss A. M. Anderson, Sunnybrae, Pitlochry

E RASPBERRY ACID

6 lb. ripe raspberries
$2\frac{1}{2}$ oz. tartaric acid
granulated sugar

Dissolve tartaric acid in 2 pints cold water and pour over fruit. Let it stand for 24 hours, then drain liquid off without pressing fruit.
To every pint of juice add $1\frac{1}{2}$ lb. granulated sugar, and stir until sugar is dissolved. Bottle, do not cork, but tie linen over bottles. Keep in fridge.
Add water to taste. As an iced drink on a hot day this is superb and children love it.

Passed down in family since the last century
Mrs F. S. Johnson, Keltneyburn

LEMONADE

4 lemons
4 lbs. sugar
2 oz. citric acid
5 pints boiling water

Remove the rind from the lemons and put in a large bowl with sugar, citric acid and lemon squeezings.
Infuse with the boiling water.
Allow to cool, strain and bottle. Dilute to taste.

10 mins

Grandmother's recipe
Mrs Hubert Strathairn, Crieff

ELDERFLOWER SUMMER DRINK

4 large heads of elder flowers
1 gallon cold water
$1\frac{1}{4}$ lb. sugar
2 tablespoons wine vinegar
juice and rind of 2 lemons

Mix all together. Leave to stand for 24 hours, then bottle. Leave for 2 days before drinking.

Mrs John Mills, Barnetby, Lincs

'. . . the very Spice of Life'

Ministers there should be. Doctors and lawyers? Yes;
To each of these occasionally confess.
But, first and last, keep this advice in mind –
Good cooks, good cooking – these must save mankind.

Miss M. Douglas, Ballinluig

* * *

Lettuce will keep crisp for days in the fridge if put in a bowl with cold water (about 2″ water is enough).

Mrs D. Henderson, Aberfeldy

* * *

To mend china: Take a piece of flint glass, heat it to a fine powder, and grind it extremely fine on a painter's stone with the white of an egg. It joins china without riveting, so that no art can break it in the same place. (Household hint dated 1893)

Mrs Barbara Liddell, Pitlochry

* * *

It is popularly believed that **paraffin** is good for cleaning piano keys. It may make them look nice but if you actually want to *play* the thing you might as well use marmalade. The same is true of typewriters.

Ronald Mavor, Edinburgh

* * *

When weighing syrup, weigh pan first, and pour syrup into pan and weigh again.

Anon

The Harness Cask: a good way to keep meat without a deep freeze. Half fill a cask or Poly dustbin with fresh or salt water. Add one raw potato and spoon in coarse salt until the potato floats. The liquid will preserve rolled beef off the bone, or pork, for several months. It is better if it is reasonably fat free, and should be soaked in three changes of fresh water on the day before cooking.

This is far better than anything you get out of a tin, and a tough old beast becomes quite tender; however, sheep or lamb does not work so well.

Adam Kennedy Bergius, Helensburgh

* * *

To prevent a skin forming on custard, sprinkle with a fine layer of castor sugar.

Anon

* * *

To clean silver: Soak a clean dry glass cloth in the following mixture:

2 tablespoons methylated spirit
1 level dessertspoon Goddard's plate powder
1 teacup cold water

Dry cloth and shake well. Wash silver in hot water. Dry while hot and wet with the above cloth.

Anon

* * *

Pick raspberries straight into boxes that can be put into the freezer. In this way they will only be touched once. When defrosting turn out on to large dish so that berries are not on top of each other.

Lady Balfour of Burleigh, Clackmannan

Croutons are very popular and most useful for adding to soups, but they are a nuisance when they have to be made, in addition to everything else, at the last minute before a dinner party. They freeze beautifully. Fry an entire large sliced loaf, put into several polythene bags when cool, and use as needed. They will not stick together in a frozen state, and can be shaken out of the bag and heated in the oven just before serving soup.

Mrs John Horsfall, Kinloch Rannoch

* * *

For sticky hands after a picnic, take with you, in a wide-necked vacuum flask or other container, ice cubes from the fridge or freezer. One of these in the hands for a moment or two will remove all stickiness. Dry on a napkin or piece of kitchen towel.

Anon

* * *

Pancakes freeze beautifully. Make them in the usual way, and freeze with a piece of greaseproof paper between each one.

Mrs Barbara Liddell, Pitlochry

* * *

A quick and simple **chocolate sauce** that children love: Melt a Mars bar with a tablespoon of milk slowly over a gentle heat and pour over ice cream or fruit.

Anon

* * *

Coming home from Spain with your **duty free brandy,** spare one for 1 jar of sultanas and 1 jar of glacé cherries. Add to each jar 2 cloves, 2 strips of lemon peel, small piece of cinnamon stick, and top up with the brandy. Ready for all your Christmas baking and puddings.

Mrs Turk, Fasganeon Hotel, Pitlochry

* * *

To boil rhubarb and water together in an aluminium pan will really clean the pan.

Anon

* * *

To remove air from plastic bags: when packed with fruit or veg for the freezer, simply hold the top of the bag in one hand and submerge bag in bucket of water until all air has escaped. Tie with tape.

Mrs R. S. Stewart-Wilson, Tullymet

* * *

Vinegar has many uses:

Restoring whiteness of porcelain: Yellowed porcelain such as ranges and refrigerators can be restored to white if washed with hot vinegar.

Cleaning brass and copper: Make a paste of white vinegar, salt and flour. Rub utensils with this paste, then polish with oil to prevent tarnishing.

Relieving wasp stings: Cider vinegar applied to a wasp sting will relieve the alkaline poison injected by the wasp.

Relieving sunburn: Apply white vinegar with sponge. This will give relief.

To clean salad greens: Insects and bugs on greens, lettuce and vegetables come to the surface if left standing for about 10 minutes in a solution of 1 part vinegar to 5 parts water.

Fabric stain remover: A little vinegar rubbed on colourfast clothes will remove grease, perspiration, water and scorch stains.

Cleaning paint brushes: Dried paint brushes can be cleaned by letting the brush stand simmering in white vinegar for 10 minutes.

Care for nylon stockings: Stockings and tights will last longer and retain their lustre if rinsed in cold water to which a small amount of white vinegar has been added.

Mrs T. G. Donald, Pitlochry

* * *

To prevent top of cooker becoming brown with long hot cooking like jam making, rub with butter before beginning cooking.

Anon

* * *

Never eat an **orange** or use a **lemon** without grating the peel. The peel of one fruit, mixed with 2 tablespoons of granulated sugar and stored in a jar, can be topped up many times and used to give added flavour in puddings, biscuits and cakes. It even brightens up any ordinary custard.

Mrs Turk, Fasganeon Hotel, Pitlochry

* * *

To dry the inside of a decanter: After washing, fill it with fairly hot water. Hold it upside down under the hot tap and let the water run on the base until it is empty. Then, still holding it upside down, wrap it in a dry towel quickly, and rub it dry on the outside – and the inside dries as well. This worked with milk bottles too before we took to plastic bags!

The Misses Audrey and Jean Wright, Dunalastair

Any **left-over wine** can be frozen in a small container and used for cooking later. This is handy when a recipe requires a small amount, and saves opening a bottle.

Mrs D. Henderson, Aberfeldy

* * *

To wash woollens, mix together: ½ pint methylated spirit, ½ lb. soap flakes, 3 dessertspoons eucalyptus oil. Mix thoroughly together to a consistency similar to that of bread sauce. Keep in a tightly closed jar.

Use 1 tablespoon to ½ gallon of warm water. Wash garment (jumper, tweed skirt, etc.) in the usual way by squeezing. *Do not rinse – squeeze out surplus water.* Hang out to dry. This preserves woollen garments for years.

Mrs Hastie Smith, Comrie

* * *

To wash blankets I use the same mix. I put them in the washing machine in hand hot water. I give them a short wash but *no rinse.* Spin them dry. There is no shrinking, and they dry light and fluffy and mothproof.

Mrs Barbara Liddell, Pitlochry

* * *

A painless way of cooking **Patna rice:** Put rice into a measuring jug, noting the mark on measure to which it comes. Have a kettle on the boil, and a saucepan ready with a lid. Put a little fat in pan and melt. Add rice, coating every grain by shaking the pan a little. This is to fry or glaze the rice a *very* little. Lift pan away from heat, add 2 measures of boiling water. Return to heat, boil slowly for 12 mins. Stir once. Add a little salt before water is all gone.
N.B. Measure of water must be exact.

Mrs M. Mackenzie Smith, Enochdhu

Keep a bag of **ice cubes** in the freezer, which you have previously made in the fridge and put in bags. It is then so easy to add a cube or two to a drink when needed.

Mrs R. Begg, Bearsden

* * *

Glacé cherries, if bought in bulk and divided into small cream cartons, will freeze beautifully. They thaw quickly and never become crystallised.

Mrs C. W. Grant, Pitlochry

* * *

To Cure a Sore Throat or a Quinsey: Take the flower of Holly-hocks, boyle them in water, a good handful, drink some of the water and bind the flower to the neck, also. This cured a horse that was given over.

From the recipe book of Elizabeth Lucas Pinckney, wife of Chief Justice Charles Pinckney, Charleston, South Carolina, U.S.A. A.D. 1756.

Mrs R. Murray, Aberfeldy

* * *

To remove fluff from velvet, etc. wind cellotape round hand with sticky side outside. This collects the bits very easily.

Mrs N. Jackson, Strathtay

* * *

After liquidising **food for babies,** pour into ice cube tray and freeze. Remove cubes when frozen and put in a container or bag and keep in freezer. Remove only the number of cubes required for a meal and heat.

Mrs D. Henderson, Aberfeldy

Horseradish eaten two or three times a day after influenza cures cough and its after effects. (Old remedy dated 1893).

Mrs Barbara Liddell, Pitlochry

* * *

For a delicious sauce to serve with fish, make a good white sauce and add mashed pickled walnuts.

Mrs John Horsfall, Kinloch Rannoch

* * *

Bread dough rises very slowly in the fridge. 3 lbs. of dough can be made up at once and put in a container – a 1-gallon ice cream container is ideal. Enough can then be taken out when needed to make rolls or loaves, which are much nicer when freshly baked each time.

Mrs Kirby, Balrobin Hotel, Pitlochry

* * *

Grated cheese keeps excellently in the freezer. It is much quicker to grate 2 or 3 lbs. at once and it can be spooned out when frozen.

Mrs Kirby, Balrobin Hotel, Pitlochry

* * *

Dr. Carson's receipt **to relieve Thirst:** One ounce of wormwood to one pint of water. Take a wine glass four times daily. When weather is cold put in quietly a table spoon of whisky.

From an Old Philadelphia recipe.

Mrs R. Murray, Aberfeldy

Chocolate leaves make a very attractive decoration for mousses, roulades and other cold puddings. Pick and wash clean rose leaves of small or medium size, preferably ones with a short stem to act as a handle. Melt a small amount of plain chocolate (a little goes a long way) and, with a pastry brush, coat the underside of each leaf. They will dry very quickly, whereupon apply a second coating of chocolate. Lie them on greaseproof paper on a board and leave them in the fridge until completely cold.

On removing them from the fridge, lever them off the greaseproof paper and, holding the stem, peel the leaf off the chocolate. It is most important not to try to peel the chocolate from the leaf as it will most certainly break. The leaves will be veined and each one an exact replica of the original – and they are extremely easy and quick to make.

Mrs John Horsfall, Kinloch Rannoch

* * *

Experience shows that babies will eat anything if it is in a white sauce.

Lady Balfour of Burleigh, Clackmannan

* * *

Prunes are delicious washed, put in pan, covered with water, brought to the boil, and put in a wide-mouthed vacuum flask with the water. Even better boiled, then put in small jar, covered with dry sherry and left in fridge for about a week.

Mrs Kirby, Balrobin Hotel, Pitlochry

* * *

A spoonful *very cold* water added to **cream** while whipping will reduce the chance of it turning to butter and also makes it keep fresher for longer.

Mrs John Cameron, Blair Atholl

Remedy for Cystitis: *Elder flowers.* Pick elder flower heads when very dry, and dry them in a paper bag. When they are brown, rub them together to get rid of stems. Use one tablespoon of the powder in a cup of boiling water, and drink as tea.

Mrs Barbara Liddell, Pitlochry

* * *

If **kitchen tools** need oiling, apply a little glycerine with an eyedropper. If any accidentally gets into food don't worry. It is harmless.

Miss M. Douglas, Ballinluig

* * *

Parsley should be much used in cooking – being a very wholesome herb, and *very good for anaemia.* (Old remedy dated 1893).

Mrs Barbara Liddell, Pitlochry

* * *

A teaspoon of sugar added to vegetables with the salt while they are cooking much improves the flavour.

Mrs John Cameron, Blair Atholl

* * *

Mint sauce concentrate: 2 tablespoons golden syrup (or more if much mint). All the mint from the garden, finely chopped. Melt the syrup over gentle heat, slowly stir in the chopped mint. Keep stirring in the mint until the syrup will take no more.

Pour into jars. To reconstitute, take a spoonful of mint syrup and add vinegar to taste. Truly Fresh Mint Sauce Flavour.

Anon

* * *

Make **hollandaise sauce** in a blender with liquid butter. This saves hours of precious time stirring in nuts of softened butter.

Mrs Walter Steuart Fothringham, Dunkeld

* * *

Always **roast chicken, partridge or grouse** upside down. It keeps the breast beautifully moist.

Mrs Walter Steuart Fothringham, Dunkeld

* * *

Profiterole cases freeze beautifully, and can be quickly filled with either a sweet or savoury mixture. If this is done before the cases defrost it makes them much easier to handle.

Mrs Walter Steuart Fothringham, Dunkeld

* * *

I once tried making lasagne without cooking the pasta first, but put it in raw with the layers of Bolognese and béchamel sauces. It seemed to work just as well as the tedious business of cooking three pieces of pasta at a time and drying it. However it took slightly longer to cook it.

Mrs P. B. Hay, Comrie

* * *

CONVERSION TABLES

OVEN TEMPERATURES

	Degrees Fahrenheit	*Regulo*	*Degrees Centigrade*
Very slow	200-280	$\frac{1}{4}$-$\frac{1}{2}$	115-135
Slow	280-320	1	135-160
Warm	320-340	3	160-170
Moderate	340-370	4	170-185
Fairly hot	370-400	5-6	185-205
Hot	400-440	7	205-225
Very hot	440-500	8-9	225-250

* * *

Standard measuring cup	= $\frac{1}{2}$ pint
$\frac{1}{4}$ cup liquid	= 4 tablespoons
$\frac{1}{2}$ cup liquid	= 1 gill
$\frac{1}{2}$ cup butter	= 1 stick
2 cups butter	= 1 lb.
5 cups freshly grated cheese	= 1 lb.
2 cups cottage cheese	= 1 lb.
2 level tablespoons flour	= 1 oz.
4 cups flour	= 1 lb.
$2\frac{1}{3}$ cups raw rice	= 1 lb.
1 level tablespoon white sugar	= 1 oz.
2 cups white sugar	= 1 lb
$2\frac{1}{4}$ cups firmly packed brown sugar	= 1 lb.

INDEX

Copies of this recipe book may be obtained from Pitlochry Festival Theatre, price £1.25 post free.